Love Meets Life

Stories of Love Showing Up
in Unexpected Ways

Compiled by Tara Ijai

Keep choosing
love !
xoxo,
Tara 10/10/2020

Love Meets Life Stories of Love Showing Up in Unexpected Ways

As You Wish Publishing, LLC
Connect@asyouwishpublishing.com

ISBN-13: 978-1-951131-07-4
Library of Congress Control Number: 2020917105

Compiled by Tara Ijai

Printed in the United States of America.

Nothing in this book or any affiliations with this book is a substitute for medical or psychological help. If you are needing help please seek it.

Dedication

Dedicated to all the Love Rebels out there:
the badass warriors who keep choosing love
each and every time.

Love is an
Action word! 1/11/2020
Deedra

always choose
love!
Sara Ifai
11/11/2020

Table of Contents

Foreword

Why write a book about love?

I believe in the year 2020, this is exactly the kind of book we need.

When approaching the potential authors with this book idea, I didn't give them any parameters. There was no definition of what love should look like or sound like. The prompt was simple and clear: "Write about love."

I didn't want to color it with my version of what I thought love was or what it should look like. I wanted it open and vulnerable, and the authors to authentically define love in their way.

I knew that this wasn't for the faint of heart. We had several well-intentioned authors that had to drop out because they could not focus on love while in the midst of worldly chaos.

I feel we are not doing justice if we do not consider the landscape in 2020. There are so many ways hate and negativity visibly show up these days. The political rhetoric has increased exponentially and is so divisive, hate crimes are on the rise, Covid-19, a virus of global proportion is happening all over the world, affecting communities and economies, and that is not our only pandemic. I'm referring to the systematic oppression of our black community that has given birth to movements such as Black Lives Matter in the face of extreme police brutality. There are protests and marches and voices wanting to be heard. There is so much focus on the negative that it can be absolutely destructive.

In spite of this, or because of this, our authors chose to take on this task of writing about love.

Some authors jumped at the chance to write on the topic, and others were not so confident that they had something to offer or that their story would not be "right." I can assure you upon completion that all the stories are perfect because they are a creation from the hearts and souls of love rebels who are looking to make the world a better place and leave it just a little bit better than they found it.

I believe people thought that our book was solely going to be filled with stories of kittens and rainbows. While it's a beautiful visual and so deeply appreciated, I don't believe love always looks like that. I think people that went through a form of struggle or hardship and still come out on the other side shining bright like a beacon in the dark are the most epic angels on this planet. I can't think of anything more divine than showing up with love and being in service to others, especially after going through a hardship.

The authors delved deep into the depths of their souls to bring out what stories of love that they wanted to birth into the world.

Each story is so different, so unique that you can clearly see how vastly different each person chooses to show up, just like in life itself. Some share stories about family, friends, or lovers, and some share about their ideas of self-love. Some show up as the "helpers" that Mr. Rogers' mother told him about.

We know you will find something or someone to connect to in this book that will feed your soul.

Let me introduce you to the authors. I asked them to share in their words who they are in the world.

Here is how we show up. Here is who we are…

We are a young teenager to senior citizens. We are black, white, Latinx, Filipina, Irish, Canadian, Multiracial, Muslim, Christian, Jewish, Catholic, Atheist, Spiritual, non-binary, gender fluid, bisexual, and gay.

We are wives, single moms, sisters, fathers, grandparents, brothers, widows, friends, lovers, aunties, and nieces.

We are fitness coaches, speaking coaches, lawyers, judges, doctors, construction workers, tarot card readers, nurses, politicians, astrologers, librarians, business owners, entrepreneurs, birth doulas, photographers, dog rescuers, foster moms, adoptive moms and some of us are not moms at all.

We are neuro-diverse, autistic, introverted, extroverted, social justice warriors, vegan, coffee lovers, secret keepers, kindness ambassadors, yoga lovers, animal huggers, Guinness book world record huggers, artists, overachievers, cancer survivors, singers, influencers and dreamers.

This is our essence, our essence of who we are. We are you, and you are us, and we are all authors of love.

Tara Ijai is a love rebel who actively rebels against hate and negativity. She helps spread love in the world using her heart-shaped sunglasses as a tool and reminder to make the world a better place. Her passion is connecting with people one smile and conversation at a time, and she believes that love is a superpower. You can reach Tara at: www.loveglassesrevolution.com.

Love Is An Action Word
By Deedra Abboud

Love.
Love is an action word.

Commitment to sharing love in the world is a character trait. Unloving encounters are a test of your commitment to love.

Too many people have no idea how much ugliness their co-workers and neighbors experience because they don't really know them, don't have the conversations, don't witness the behavior firsthand, or worse, make excuses for the behavior in an effort to make "peace."

You're not neutral, and you're not making peace.

You're hurting people already hurting.

Being blind to toxic behavior hurts everyone.

Ignoring toxic behavior only gives it more power to hurt again.

Some of us don't have the privilege to ignore the ugliness. Ugliness searches us out, even if we try to keep ourselves invisible and not cause any waves—simply due to who we are, who we love, how we show up in the world, or whether someone assumes we would be an easy target.

I've had a lot of experience standing up for myself and others, so I've done a lot of self-reflection on what standing up with love, for love, looks like.

In early 2003, during the preparations for the second Iraq war, I decided to call into a local conservative radio show to counter the misinformation being said about Muslims. I got through. I countered with facts and statistics.

The host disconnected the call and said, on-air, that the screener would be fired if I ever got through again. For the rest of the year, the host attacked me, personally, almost every day. Any commentary against Muslims, his favorite subject, he always included my name.

By December, I was the poster child for the anti-Christmas movement in Arizona.

Many groups are offended during the Christmas season for various reasons that have little to do with Christianity itself, such as materialism and separation of church and state.

But among Muslims, being offended by Christmas celebrations is an extreme minority.

On Christmas Eve, after months of the host's malicious hounding of Muslims and me, I purchased a "Merry Christmas" cookie tin and glued every symbol associated with Christmas that I could find on it.

I drove to the station where he was live on the air, but it was a skeleton crew, and no one was in the reception area to open the door. I called one of the reporters from the station that I knew, and he arranged for my gift delivery within the hour.

The host never mentioned my gift. Nor did he ever say my name again, derogatory or otherwise. I extended the olive branch of love, and he accepted it, even if he never acknowledged it.

More recently, while running for U.S. Senate, a local Patriot group targeted my campaign, online and in real life. At an event in 2017, we asked the police to allow the protestors to remain on private property outside the event space for one hour, then escort them to the public space. They decided to leave after one hour instead of relocating to the public space. I neutralized their power to blame me for suppressing their voices. I let them be heard. Love.

Because it wasn't about me.

At an event in early 2018, we found out the Patriot group planned to crash my event at a restaurant to get us kicked out. Instead, we moved the event to a private hall and, to their astonishment, let them walk right in. Love.

They were verbally ugly, angry, and loud.

I faced them and their explosive accusations on their weaponized Facebook Live. Most attending the event had never seen people act and speak that way to another human being in real life.

While many of us (People of Color, indigenous, LGBTQ, minority religions, etc.) have experienced the hateful rhetoric firsthand for years, most of the attendees were shocked—like they were unwillingly watching a gross reality show. I wanted others to witness it so they would know this is the reality for many, sometimes daily.

Because it wasn't about me.

Later in 2018, one of the Patriot group members cornered and verbally attacked me on a public sidewalk in Phoenix.

While I stood there trapped, feeling her negative energy and hateful words seeping into my skin, her phone thrust in my face like a weapon, I instinctively decided to do the unexpected to defend myself. Over and over, I told her how much I loved her and how beautiful she was. Love.

She seems oblivious to it, but it was like Teflon for me. I felt the calm replacing the stress, and the hate stopped penetrating my soul. The video is still on YouTube: Deedra4BoS—"Love is more powerful than hate on Phoenix streets."

When the Patriot group condemned my attacker and claimed she was no longer a part of their group, because she was also arrested for vandalizing a local Mosque, I defended them. I got a lot of pushback from some liberals and progressives for my stance, but I believed it was the right thing to do, the loving thing to do.

I don't want to be blamed for the acts of others simply because we share characteristics either. I also want people to believe me when I condemn the acts of others—an expectation some have for the 1.8 billion Muslims in the world, even for those we've never met and have no association.

In each of these situations, I gave my attackers what I wanted to receive: an olive branch, to be heard, to be loved, to be defended, and to be believed.

But in none of these situations did I back down from my values.

For love to be true, it must be consistent. And part of that consistency is how you show up with love, for love, both for yourself and others. Because commitment to sharing love in the world is a character trait, even more so during unloving encounters.

Love is an action word.
Love.

Deedra Abboud is an attorney and social justice advocate in Arizona. Her passion is teaching how to have uncomfortable conversations, particularly in political environments. You can reach Deedra at
Deedra.Abboud@gmail.com.

Insert Title Here
By Linda Baumgartner

I was sitting with my grandsons trying to figure out the title of my "who knows what the hell I am going to write" story. We sat in silence, then suddenly, all three of us yelled, "Insert Title Here!" We laughed until we cried. Because the three of us and our brilliant minds together silently agreed—that is my title!

I have struggled for weeks, sitting in front of my computer, reading "how to write" books and articles, brainstorming with friends until I finally threw my hands in the air, and admitted defeat. *I can't do this!*

This morning I had a text-messenger conversation for about an hour with my sweet friend Tara! This girl is persistent! She wants us to be bound together—literally. This is my final attempt. Wish me luck!

My life adventure began when I was two months old. I traveled from Globe, Arizona to Roseburg, Oregon, on a pillow on my Grandma Della's lap. Life was simple—building forts, playing chase, climbing Mt. Nebo, fishing and rock-hounding with my Dad, playing detectives—complete with peeping into neighbors' windows and running freely through the neighborhood until dark. Each day I ran across the field, down the alley, and through the gate to Grandma Della's house. Her arms were always open, and her pantry was full of goodies. The garden smelled like heaven. One side of the house was covered with sweet peas from the ground to the roof. I loved being at Grandma's and Grandpa's. I was loved and accepted completely, and I never doubted my worth.

I learned early on that I wanted to be just like Grandma Della. I wanted to be a really supportive, loving, and fun mom. The answer to, "What do you want to be when you grow up?" was always "A *mom*!" Success—I was blessed with my three amazing kids. Then I was blessed with six fantastic grandkids. Could life get any better?

Life works in strange ways—ups, downs, and what the holy hell is happening times. Throughout my life, I have learned I am an empath who is affected by every damn thing happening. It's painful and exhausting. The people I have loved the most have caused me the most pain. My early days were filled with laughter, but as I have gotten older, they are often filled with tears. There was always hope in my heart that when I reached a certain age, I would be just like Grandma Della—bringing love and comfort to everyone I met.

Instead of the life I envisioned at this age, my days are filled with self-doubt, tears, anger, disappointment, and always feeling like I'm not enough. I need to be "fixed." Nothing I have done has been right or enough. I dream of moving away to an island and never looking back. But— those grandkids. I can't leave my grandkids.

The turbulence in the world today is magnifying every feeling I have. Darkness has become my best friend. I wake up each day, waiting for the night. This was never me, but now it is.

Many years ago, when I was going through a tough time, but determined to grow through it, my friend Margaret said when I commented on my lack of progress, "Oh you can muck around at the bottom for a long time before you get to the top of the mountain." Great! Surely, I should be near the top of the mountain by now, not mucking around at the bottom. Yet, here I am covered in mud and muck. Hopeless!

Still, I wake up every day and try to spread love and kindness to those willing to accept it. I hold onto hope—hope that the world will be sane and kind; hope that all people will be treated fairly with love, justice and kindness; hope that I will be accepted for who I am; hope that something I do or say makes the world a little better; hope that my grandkids will always feel loved and accepted for exactly who they are.

I believe our children are our future and trust they will be the change we so desperately need. I have found adults are far less likely to take a bold leap into the unknown, running wildly toward truth and light. May the children prevail! May every child grow up feeling heard, loved, and accepted. May they never lose their voice and resolve!

As for me, my soul searches to discover how to show up as the best me in the world continues. My "happy place," as verified by Meyers-Briggs, is to be around people I love and care for, and feeling an underlying loyalty and appreciation from them. Boy, they nailed it! My mantra going forward is, "I am me! I am good! I am lovable! I am enough!"

My love journey continues! Standby!

Linda Baumgartner is a love rebel and passionate believer in our children. She speaks freely with any child with the will to listen about the importance of love, inclusiveness, and kindness. Her passion is kindness. You can reach her at mygrammab@gmail.com.

True 2 U
By Thaia Bey

Hi, my name is Thaia Bey. I am the founder of nonprofit True2u. We promote self-confidence, self-love, and self-I can.

I know you are wondering how this dream came about. Well let's begin.

I was 13 when this all happened, my mind was so young and creative. I was involved with a dance company, cheer, and theater. I knew I was destined for greatness from my first standing ovation for my dance solo. I have been bullied my whole life for being talented and beautiful, inside and out. Growing up, girls were so jealous of me, and all I wanted to do was show love.

As time went on, I found myself vulnerable, not ready for the world, and looking for love in all the wrong places—how many can relate? Well, at 17, I had my first child. I decided to graduate early and go off to college for my license in phlebotomy and certified medical assisting. I knew I needed an education to provide for my son. His father was murdered at a young age, so there I was, feeling alone and wondering about true love.

At age 20, I thought I found it in another man. The only thing he brought was my three beautiful children. Unfortunately, I was stuck in an eight-year abusive relationship that I finally got strong enough to leave. Fast forward, I start living again, dancing, modeling, and runway, of course—well, after counseling and some alone time. I thought it would be different dating a man who needed some guidance. This time I was on birth control to protect myself and wanted no more surprises. Needless to say, here I was gullible and naive again, no great examples to follow. Well, surprise, I'm pregnant on birth control like, "How did this happen?" Just my luck, this man I only dated for a year is a cheater, an alcoholic, and a coke user.

All I could say to myself is, "Wow, Thaia, your ex was right, no man would ever want a woman with all your kids."

Furthermore, I created a deep, dark place of depression, unforgiveness, sadness, trust issues, low self-esteem, and feeling like all my dreams have been shattered because of all my unwise decisions. I took two years to get closer to God and more involved with the church. I thought this was the answer to take away all my pain and confusion, until I realized it was a Band-aid.

Well, I decided to start dating again, but he thought I was dumb. I saw the red flags right away. He was talking to me plus his three babies' mothers, then tried to make it seem like everything was my fault and wanted me acting like a wife before the ring—boy, please! He also had me on a scheduled day and tried to hide the fact his ex-girlfriend was living with him at one point, and the worse part was he tried to justify everything he did in God's name. Can you guys guess how long that relationship lasted considering all the trauma I been through? Let me help you answer that question of mine: six months, to be exact.

At this point in my life, I was so fed up with men, saying how overrated dating is and relationships are. I said to myself that there are no good men left, and I am officially and completely over dating. Well, guess what y'all, I was minding my business one day sitting in my godbrother's clothing store with my oldest son and daughter. This tall chocolate man walks through the door, and I swear I heard angelic music and saw a glow around this man. I know it's crazy, but I felt like I was in a movie.

I asked my brother, "Who is that?"

He answers me, "Oh, that's just David."

Well, I dove right in and introduced myself. At this point, we were having such an awesome connection, and I remember telling him that he talked a lot, and he just laughed. Needless to say, we have been glued to one another ever since. Here we are, six years later, married, and we added another princess to the crew, which now gives a total of six beautiful children. This man, my husband, King David, has always supported my dreams, my talents, my aspirations, my wants, my needs, and he always found a way to make it happen with no excuses.

Let's rewind to two years ago at the age of 34 and all my hard work is paying off—commercials, brand work, print work, short films, runway—New York fashion week was iconic. I worked so hard to be accepted as a curvy girl. You guys will never believe I was bullied in my hometown and New York because of how I looked. I am sorry, but I don't skip meals, smoke all day, and live off bean soup and salad! I love to eat. The director in New York was so mean to me because I was not a standard model, but this was the day I made a vow to help others be comfortable in their own skin and also help those less fortunate and in need. Drum roll please—this was the birth of True2u where we would show our youth, single parents, and young men and young women the importance of self-confidence, self-love and self-I can.

When I got back to my hometown, I started the process of creating a nonprofit. I shared this wonderful news two years ago, now we have volunteered, given to less fortunate, and supported college students. Six months ago, I started sewing a clothing line that is dedicated to curvy women, so be on the lookout for the True2u movement and True2u Curves. I promise to make a difference one heart at a time, and—do me a huge favor—ask yourself what does being true2u mean, and are you living your true dreams in your true body? Never stop believing! Much love you guys, until we meet again.

Thaia Bey, is wife to David Edgecombe and a mother to six beautiful children: Jacques, Jassan, Jaziah, Jhaia, Mosaya, and Gianna. She is a model, certified makeup artist, dancer, and actress. Her dream started when she was 13 years of age and became involved in dance, theater, and cheer. Thaia has touched many runways, one of those being during New York Fashion Week and many others. She also started her nonprofit True2u two years ago, where she promotes self-confidence, self-love, and self-I can.

You can follow her at:
Instagram @true2u_movement
Website: thaiabey324.wixsite.com/true2u

Be Brave
By Brad Boulrice

To truly tell this story would take well over 1,000 words, but for me, this is and always will be my favorite love story.

My name is Brad Boulrice. I live in Phoenix, Arizona, and have my own little business doing construction around town. I love it. My father, Bruce, and my mother, Judy, are living out here as well as my two older siblings, Tara and Marcy. We all migrated out here from a small village in upstate New York with about 3,800 people, and the mayor was our local barber. I loved that little town.

When I was about 17, my oldest sister moved to Phoenix and started a life. Soon, my other sister followed, as well as our parents. We have seen some of this country let me tell you with all the traveling and trips back and forth. What a country. Coming from a small town in upstate NY and growing up in that nice, rural bubble, it was not like us to quickly understand and process all of the cultural, political, and flat out bulls*%t the world had in store for us.

Fast forward to me at 20. One day, my oldest sister did something that I will never forget. She went to Morocco. She got off a plane in a foreign country all alone. She got married in the most beautiful ceremony. And she flew back a happily married woman. I always thought to myself, my sister is so brave. Oh yeah, she had also married a Muslim man and had converted to Islam awhile before all of that. But we will get to that.

14

I am the one in my family who orbits around the rest. Not just because I am a husky guy, but because it has always felt like my job to protect them ever since my late teens and into my early twenties. I have moved from Massachusetts, Arizona, Texas, California, and New York, and some of them two times or more. I don't consider myself any kind of world traveler. Still, I have seen my share of relationships, promises, lies, depression, anger, finances, health, and spiritual well-being. All of these are the daily grind for my family and close friends. As it is for everyone else's family and close friends. Why are we so scared to acknowledge that?

This story, if you haven't figured it out by now, is one that you hardly ever hear. The story of the brother of the woman, who decided to turn her life to Islam. Does that sound like a funny sitcom? I kind of like it. I liked it until most of the so-called friends and what not started having a lot to say about my older sister. You know, the one I am supposed to protect.

Well, I tell ya, this threw everything into a different path. A better path. My family has had to overcome many different obstacles regarding my sis. I say obstacles like it is some sort of problem. Well, it was. We were *unprepared*. We were not used to this kind of lifestyle and idea. We only heard what we heard from other people living in our glorious happy rural bubble. And mind you, we have been at some sort of war with Islam since I can remember. I mean, at least that's what the news said. Always. The most I knew about Islam was what my father, a Commanding Officer, told me—they stick to themselves, and they showed great respect to my father in bad situations. The news and locals would read a few excerpts from the "Koran for dummies" and sometimes give their profound views as well (easiest way to clear your Facebook friends list, by the way).

I was not taught racism. But I have felt it, and I have dealt with it. I carry shame for that, in the form of trying to be a better man. To help people in society that actually need it. My sister taught me that. Not the better man part. The part I told you about earlier. About how damn brave I said she was. That taught me over the years by watching her that I, too, can be brave. Have you ever seen someone flip off your sister and call her the most disgusting, foul things that you can imagine? Well, I have. The old me would just want to tear the car door off and slap these people.

But the person that my sister has helped me become just allows me to be the better person. To try to help these people understand that religion, politics, family, and whatever other human dignities they think are getting trampled on by a Muslim woman picking up organic chicken breast at Sprouts is just not her intention. We all want to be brave and love strong, but we don't always want to stand out on that limb alone. My sister taught me to jump on the edge of that limb and see where the fall takes me.

In summary, I just want to say I am a truly happy man today. I have the perfect dysfunctional family. I have a beautiful fiancé and three beautiful stepchildren I will always be proud to call my own. My sisters have two boys and a beautiful girl, and we all have our health. We argue like there is no tomorrow, and we love the same. We try our very best to understand and appreciate one another because tomorrow is not guaranteed. I write this because I don't know if I say it enough. I finally fell in love with the person I have always looked past, put down, ridiculed, shamed, and tried to avoid dealing with at all costs. Me. Pardon me while I get back to living this love story y'all.

Brad Boulrice is a local contractor that believes what goes around comes around. He treats each client how he would like to be treated. His passion is innovating and creating new projects and ideas. You can reach him and his fully loaded work trailer ready to go at:
Good Karma Construction Email: GKCBuilt@gmail.com

When A Whisper Becomes A Roar
By Jen Buck

We'd been in the car for fifteen grueling hours. Fifteen hours of dark gray, ominous skies. Fifteen hours of big, dusty, rolling nothingness. While I love Texas, driving through west Texas and into Arizona can be terribly bland and exhaustingly long. Did I mention it was fifteen hours?

We had finally gotten home, unloaded, and unpacked from that marathon drive. We'd just settled into our pajamas and I noticed that my phone notifications had blown up in the half-hour since we'd walked in the door. Every platform that people could reach me through was lit up like chickenpox, red dots covering my entire phone screen. Logic and practicality told me to ignore it at that hour but something whispered that I couldn't let it be. I saw message after message from people trying to contact me to help out with some refugees.

"Refugees? What does that even mean?" my partner John asked me. I didn't have an answer for that but I was pulling a sweatshirt over my pajamas and throwing on socks and tennis shoes, with a plan to help out any way I could. As I was driving down to the location, I was on autopilot mode. I wasn't sure what was whispering for me to take action but I could sense something big. And, I certainly wasn't sure what I was specifically being called to do, but I knew intuitively that I had to do this.

When I arrived at the church around 10:00 at night, a hundred people were strewn about. These families were

Central American asylum seekers who had been dropped off, after being lawfully released from ICE and Border Patrol custody. There were limp, exhausted parents with heads down on tables, babies crying, stressed mothers nursing, and wired, happy kids running amok everywhere. The joy being expressed by the playful kids created an emotional distortion amid the backdrop of the adults who looked confused, frightened, and shell-shocked, after many weeks in custody and a harrowing months-long journey on foot. I'm usually a great read on people and situations. Still, every alarm bell in me was going off, creating dizziness from the intensity. What in the world could I do to help here? What made me think I should come down? Who am I to do this?

In the middle of my empathic overload, a woman broke me from my emotional whirlwind. She said hurriedly, "Are you here to take a family for the night?" and without missing a beat I said, "I'll take two families." Within a few minutes of blurred paperwork and fuzzy instructions, I had two fathers and their sons in my car, and we were navigating through the dark streets of central Phoenix. Now, there's something you need to know about me: I'm a talker. I'm a bonder. I'm a caretaker. I'm your "hostess with the mostest." So, as we were driving from the church, I was doing my best to be all of that to my guests in the car. But, the truth was, I was a frantic mess of senseless chatter, radio fumbling, awkward smiles, and clunky high school Spanish that was not hitting the mark. It was all wrong. I was all wrong, and I could see it from the worried and distressed looks on their faces. I knew that my singular goal of putting them at ease and making them feel welcome was not happening.

The next morning, after worrying all night about them, I awoke to smiling, well-rested, and trusting faces who were ready to bond, enjoy, and *eat*. We ate, we played, we ate some more, we used Google Translate to communicate, and we connected in our four short hours together before we had to go to the airport. One of the fathers, Martin, didn't communicate much with me. I could tell that he was shy, and his teenage son did most of the enthusiastic sharing. But, still, everything felt like it was in Technicolor. It all felt heightened—the stories brought on more emotion. The play seemed more joyous. The bonding seemed deeper. Thinking back, those four hours felt like days, somehow. It was all so raw and real.

At the airport, I could feel a familiar pain arise. It was the kind of pain when you have to say goodbye to someone you will never see again. It was ominous, and I became somewhat slow-moving, dreading the moment when I would have to let go. I dropped the first family at the gate and felt gut-punched as I walked away, stifling sobs that were barely held in. Then, it was time to say goodbye to Martin and his son. I hugged the fifteen-year-old boy tightly, while my heart screamed in pain. This kid was the epitome of the American Dream. Then, Martin stepped up shyly and grabbed my face tenderly with both hands and whispered, in perfect but shaky English, "I love you, lady."

I love you, lady.

My world tilted at that very moment. Life came to a screeching halt, and things were suddenly slamming into clarity. It was then that I realized I was being ordered to do something much greater than I had ever done. And, it wasn't a whisper that was directing me, it was a roar.

Since that very day, I have followed the roar. I have founded a nonprofit that aids asylum seekers who are fleeing violence in their countries. We provide clothing, food, medical care, family hosting, transportation, translation, and travel services. Everything that I did for my two families is now being done by over 700 volunteers who are experiencing the same life-changing feeling that I did, as they help us with our families. We've contributed in one way or another in helping over 45,000 people get reunited with their families and on their way to legal citizenship, which has been the single greatest honor of my life.

And all of this because of a whisper of love.

Jen Buck is a professional speaker and founder of a nonprofit organization. She's spoken to countless numbers of people and has been a speaker for the largest corporations in the world, for over 20 years. Her career began at a start-up, and she now teaches and coaches leadership strategies to high-performing organizations and leaders. She believes that when we are in service to others and actively leading for the common good, we are able to tap into a heightened level of influence, which inspires immeasurable acts of greatness. You can contact her at jenbuckspeaks.com.

The Harp, The Heart, And The Brain
By Rev. Dr. Joyce Buekers

According to the Associated Press, Americans spend over thirty billion dollars annually on complementary medicine. People are looking for more options and compassionate, healthier alternatives to the damaging effects of drugs and surgeries.

I believe that effective healthcare must encompass both the art of a loving heart tied into the science of medicine. The heart, the brain, and the harp together—all three use neurons that make a difference in our health and well-being.

I grew up in an artistic family of musicians on my mother's side and a science-based engineering family on my father's side. My grandmother was a world-renowned harpist who played for Disney Studios for forty years, most memorably as a harpist in the movie Fantasia. She inspired my mother, my sisters, my daughter, and I to follow in her harp playing footsteps. After receiving my master's in business while minoring in music in college, I was not sure which direction to take when I started my career—art or science. My father convinced me that the computer field was more lucrative than music, and I was hired as the first woman in sales for the IBM Data Processing Division in Phoenix in the 1970s.

A successful career at IBM ended when a semi-truck rear-ended my car in January of 1991, and my entire life changed. My jaw was broken, seven vertebrae were damaged, my brain was severely rattled—these were the physical effects of the accident. Emotionally, my children lost the support of their mother, and my marriage was wobbled. I had lost the career I had built at IBM. I felt broken, physically, and emotionally.

For too long, I was not functional. I saw seventeen specialists, had seven hundred and thirty-five doctor's appointments, and three orthoscopic surgeries to my jaw. While meditating during these difficult times, at a time when I needed peace, the idea of love versus fear-based models of medicine came to me. Our healthcare system was based on diagnostics, surgeries, and drugs, and this created a fear-based system. Very little of what I was going through was centered on love, compassion, or caring.

I started meeting doctors whose practices centered on both science and spirituality. We found an integrative medicine practice at Cedar Sinai in Los Angeles that would help to fix my brain injury, concussion, and jaw. I was learning neuroscience, and the power of using energy to heal, the spiritual side of healthcare. Neurons that fire together, wire together. I listened to music, visualizations, and meditations, and became mindful of where my pain was centralized within my body. The doctors would then go in and arthroscopically scrape the joint where the disc was displaced. My mind knew what to do to start the healing process—allowing for the electromagnetic brain to take over where the doctors' scalpels had stopped. I had an awakening as to what was needed to heal.

During the healing process, the doctors asked what had brought me joy and peace previous to the accident. I thought of our family's history with the harp and sat in my living room, teaching myself again how to play. In retrospect, rather than this accident being the worst experience of my life, the accident brought me back to my family's legacy of harp playing and created a new direction for my career.

A new focus started with the harp playing, an awakening to a new purpose through my healthcare experiences, which all lead to my call to Healthcare Ministry. I started the Integrative Therapies Program at Hospice of the Valley. I founded a non-profit organization, the Therapeutic Harp Foundation. The Foundation delivers the power of live therapeutic harp to healthcare settings. What I learned through my experience is that loving thoughts become a reality, and the power of a single note can transform an individual. We play for babies coming off opioids in the hospital and watch as a single note can steady heart monitors and deliver peace. Not only the babies but their families, their doctors, their nurses, their volunteers all feel this difference. We are now clinically proving how the vibration and sounds of the harp strings allow everyone to take a moment to pause, to take a breath, to feel their bodies return to a loving, balanced, centered state.

There is a growing body of scientific evidence demonstrating the link between mental and emotional attitudes, physiological health, and long-term well-being. Over sixty percent of primary care doctor visits are related to stress. Yet, only three percent of patients receive stress management help. Studies show that middle-aged people who practice mindfulness and meditative self-regulation were up to fifty times more likely to be alive and without chronic disease fifteen years later than those with lower self-regulation practices.

Our brain, the cerebral cortex, is a primary sensory organ receptive to both internal and external electromagnetic stimuli that play a crucial role in highly developed and distinctly human traits. The frequencies generated while playing harp music can help to reset the neural loops, and we can re-center and find our true selves. Working with thousands of patients, I have seen the power of energy and specifically the power of live therapeutic harp music in healthcare settings to help find peace for those who listen.

Imagine a premature baby in the intensive care unit at a hospital coming out of open-heart surgery, hearing therapeutic harp music, and watching their blood pressure and heart rate resume to normal levels. Imagine a loved one at the end of life transitioning as they allow their body to relax while listening to harp music. Imagine yourself in the hospital, listening to a loving alternative such as therapeutic harp and healing quicker with less pain medicine. I am excited about the future of medicine and how the frequencies of a love-based healthcare system can open up the heart, the brain, and transform lives.

The Rev. Dr. Joyce Buekers was ordained in Phoenix at the Church of the Beatitudes after a successful marketing career with IBM Corporation. Joyce's second career in healthcare ministry was inspired by her experience as the Integrative Therapies Coordinator with Hospice of the Valley, where Joyce founded the Therapeutic Harp

Foundation in 2000. Dr. Buekers' passion for clinically proving the efficacy of the spiritual side of healthcare led to a recent publication in the *International Journal of Science and Engineering*, "Electromagnetic Loop Theory—A New Paradigm in Consciousness Research." Joyce married her childhood sweetheart, Michael, in 1976 and has two married adult children and one grandchild.

Soul Sister
By Patricia Burlison

It was the summer of 1980 when my family of four moved into our new home in Westminster, California. It took days to move in. I asked daddy when we were going to be able to stay the night. I remember his answer vividly. "Tonight," he said. I couldn't believe it. That night I knelt down to pray to give thanks. As I was on my knees facing my bed, I put my hands together and said, "Dear Jesus." Before I can say much more, Daddy walks in. He asked what I was doing, and I jumped up and said, "Nothing." That night I went to bed without finishing my prayer.

Just like all the other kids in a new neighborhood, my sister and I met some friends. Lorie, Poppy, and Nicole became our new best friends. We started school soon after. My older sister always walked with me to make sure I made it to school and home safely. She didn't care if her classmates made fun of her. She took care of her little sister. Daddy worked, and Mom was a homemaker. Life couldn't get any better.

Fast forward to the summer of 1981. August 8th started out normal. I was fighting with my sister, and she and Lorie went to the store. Mom decided to go to the store as well. I was playing at Poppy's waiting for them. We went outside, and some kids told us that someone was hit by a vehicle and the person they were with called her parents. Lorie didn't know our phone number, so I knew it wasn't one of them.

Poppy's mom sent me home after a while. Mom finally got home. My sister Kathleen wasn't with her, though. I was so confused. Mom summoned me over and told me to sit down. I slowly sat and just looked at her. All she said was, "She's gone." As tears ran down my face, I didn't say a single word. At that moment, I was weighed down with guilt that, to this day, has never diminished.

Before I knew it, we were packing up the house and moving to Arizona. I cried while saying goodbye to all my friends, then we drove off. Arizona was a safe place to start over. We had family there, Mom's twin sister, so all was going to be okay.

Life was difficult that year. There was no more laughter or playing with friends. I didn't ask for anything or want anything except for my sister back. I needed to tell her I was sorry for fighting with her. I needed to tell her I loved her. I just needed her to come back to heal my broken heart.

Mom and Daddy were struggling too. The new family of three grieved in our different ways. Mom turned to vodka, and Daddy didn't talk to anybody. Mom and I took Daddy to the airport to catch his flight to Oregon one day, and we didn't see him again until years later. It was just Mom, and I now trying to survive.

School was hard. I couldn't concentrate. I was in fourth grade, and the entire year in school was a blur. My teacher knew my situation and was understanding with mom. She told my Mom that I lacked attention and that I was there physically but not emotionally. It was decided not to advance me to the fifth grade. I was devastated and embarrassed. How was I going to face my classmates after that?

Since Mom was now raising me on her own we didn't have a choice but to move again. This move took us to my grandmother's in Northern California. Mom and Grand-mother weren't getting along, so on June 28, 1982, on my tenth birthday, we left her house. We drove south, not knowing where we were going to go. After driving for about eight hours, we ended up at her cousin's house in Lomita, California. We were there for a couple days until my uncle took us in. So, we headed to Anaheim.

I was grateful to Uncle Michael for helping us in our time of need. I still didn't talk much, but I felt safe in his home. After a while, my sadness turned to anger, and I wanted to die. I thought that by not finishing that prayer of gratitude in 1980, I caused the domino effect of the bad that was happening to my family. Mom eventually found work and enrolled me in fourth grade at Lincoln Elementary. That's where I met her.

I walked into Mrs. York's classroom, and there she was. This thin, beautiful, perfectly dressed nine-year-old named Denise. She had long, thick, dirty blonde hair with piercing large blue eyes. She was kind with a tender heart. We became instant friends.

It took me a while to open up to her, and we fought constantly. My heart was still broken, and my anger started showing. The more kindness Denise showed me, the angrier I got. I couldn't understand why. I really liked her and wanted to be her friend, but I took all my anger and resentment out on her. I don't know why she would want to be my friend.

After a couple years, she was able to open my heart to love. I was sixteen before I was able to speak freely about the death of my sister without crying. Denise did that. She helped me through my grief process. She showed me a love only a sister can give. She taught me about unconditional love and that you don't have to be bound by blood to be bound by souls. She made me want to live. Honestly, she saved my life.

Denise and I have been best friends for thirty-eight years, and it took me about twenty-five years to realize God sent her to me. He took my blood sister and, in return, sent me my soul sister.

Patricia Burlison is a political activist and the current Chairman of Democracy for America-Maricopa County, residing in Phoenix, Arizona. She holds a Master's Degree in Business Administration and currently works in public health. In her free time, she enjoys watching the Los Angeles Dodgers, traveling the world, and entertaining family and friends with her adult son, Sabastian. She can be reached at patricia.burlison@hotmail.com.

Be Excellent To Each Other
By Michelle Clark

Great joy was found in buying coffee for the person behind him. He loved to brighten a stranger's day with a random act of kindness. He just loved being helpful. He volunteered as an EMT for the local roller derby. He was always ready to help friends, family, and strangers alike. This brought him joy. Andy was 6'2" with the most beautiful eyes, an easy laugh, and a big heart. We met in high school and became fast friends. Fast forward about 20 years, and we were married with our first child. Life was good. Life was amazing. Life was most excellent.

All of that changed in February of 2014 when Andy passed away. It should be of no surprise that Andy's kindness also translated into being a registered organ donor. It is something we talked about, and we were in agreement that we both wanted to help as many people as we could. At the time, I didn't know that I would be making these final decisions so soon. I made the decision to follow Andy's organ donation wishes with our 16-month-old daughter on my hip.

Even in death, Andy was the most excellent human he could be. He donated his organs to five people. Our little family was forever changed. Our world came to a screeching halt. I was in complete shock that the world had the nerve to keep spinning. Didn't everyone know that the love of my life was gone? He was now stardust. Stardust. How was I going to parent our child and make sure she knew her father? How was I going to teach her all of the things she needed to know about him? How could I share all of his goodness, kindness, and love?

> "Grief, I've learned, is really just love. It's all the love you want to give but cannot. All that unspent love gathers up in the corners of your eyes, the lump in your throat, and in that hollow part of your chest. Grief is just love with no place to go." ~ Jamie Anderson

Grief is always there. It doesn't go away. You don't work through it and one day find yourself magically on the other side. You are always swimming through it. You just find better techniques, and you learn a few new strokes along the way. Helping a young child work through grief is hard work. You can't push through it to get to the end because there is no end. It just becomes different. I wanted to focus some of that grief on the good things. I wanted to focus on love.

Andy had a lifetime of good deeds left to do. We just needed a little help to keep those good deeds going in the community. How would I do that? I wanted our daughter to know what kind of person her dad was. I wanted her to have a strong connection. I had an idea. My solution was a simple business card with a quote from the movie, *Bill & Ted's Excellent Adventure*. This quote happened to be one of the last Facebook posts that Andy made, "Be Excellent To Each Other," and it became our family motto. This motto became a positive reminder of the kind of man Andy was. It is a daily reminder of who we want to be. We continue Andy's kindness, and we encourage others to do the same. It is just part of who we are as a family.

The Be Excellent Project became a Facebook page and a place to share kindness with others and encourage others to "Be Excellent" and spread the kindness in Andy's name. Be Excellent cards were sent out all across the country to encourage others to do random acts of kindness. Our friends and family started doing random acts of kindness in Andy's name. Strangers started doing random acts of kindness in Andy's name. It was rewarding to watch the ripple effect of kindness and love.

I wrote letters to the recipients of Andy's organs. I wanted to let families know that not only did they receive a life-saving act of kindness, but that it came from an amazing, kind, and loving person. I wanted them to know that Andy was kind and that he was an amazing father, that he was strong, smart, and witty. I included Be Excellent cards with my letter and sent them off.

One day a comment popped up on the Be Excellent Facebook page from someone who said they were the recipient of Andy's heart. I held my breath for a moment, and then I quickly replied. A year later, we meet in person, and I got to hear Andy's heart beating strong. Our daughter got to hear her daddy's heart beating. It was a surreal moment. Andy would have thought the whole thing was cool and would have rambled on about the science and all of the things that need to go right for a successful transplant. The Be Excellent Project brought us together. Andy brought us together. Now our lives are full of even more love as our family has grown to include them. The kindness continues to spread thanks to Andy. He would be proud.

Do you want to help spread excellence in Andy's name? We sure hope you do. It is simple. Be excellent and go out and spread kindness in Andy's name. Drop by the Be Excellent Project on Facebook and share a little kindness. Sign up to be an organ donor and tell your family your wishes. Stand up for kindness and love wherever you can and in as many ways as you can. It can be something as simple as a smile or giving a compliment. It could be making a donation to an organization. It could be volunteering or helping a neighbor.

Get creative and spread the love.

Be excellent to each other.

We love you, Andy.

Michelle Clark is a widow, mother, and lover of root beer. She claims the title of the "World's Okayest Mom." She runs the Be Excellent Project in memory of her witty and amazing husband, Andy, which encourages acts of kindness to help make the world a better place. Her mission is to complete the lifetime of kindness Andy had left to give. You can reach Michelle at https://www.facebook.com/beexcellentproject/.

Activism Is Love On Steroids
By K.C. Cooper

L ove is an action word, and activism is one of the greatest ways one can demonstrate it. To step aside from your normal routine and take vigorous action to support a cause is a very noble thing to do. It takes a lot of bravery to stand up against an opposing party and fight for justice on behalf of others.

As an African American female, I had already become a victim of police brutality by the age of fifteen. Shortly after moving to a small city east of Los Angeles, my sister and I witnessed police officers harassing some of our neighbors. They were considered cholos (young Mexican American gang members). It was dark, and our bedroom window faced the parking garage in the back of the apartments. After hearing lots of noise, we opened the window and watched through the screen, as police officers pushed and shoved the young men around. We could not help but respond with "Ooohs" and "Awwws" until a shadow flashed across the bottom of the screen, and our eyes began to burn. We immediately rushed to the bathroom to flush our eyes out with water. By the time we returned to the window, everyone was gone.

A short time after that incident, a group of police officers decided to raid our apartment late one night. The warrant (if valid or real) was supposed to be for guns and drugs. My mother was and has been a nurse all of my life, and my stepfather worked in a food supply warehouse. They took care of his elderly uncle, and me, who were home during this time. They brought everyone into the living room and proceeded to handcuff the adults. I told the officer who was placing cuffs on my mom, "Let her put some clothes on." That's when the leader of the group said, "She's the ringleader. Take her too!" So, I was handcuffed, put in the back of a police car, and taken to the police station. I was fingerprinted and had my mugshot taken before being placed in a cold cell with no blanket, pillow, or mattress. I sat there for hours until my aunt came to get me. I learned many years later that it was the first step to putting me in the system and labeling me with a prior offense.

When we made it home, I told my mother that I did not want to live in California anymore. I was born in Arizona, and that was the environment I preferred to live in. She called my aunt and made arrangements for me to move back as soon as possible. I immediately felt a sigh of relief upon my arrival. I finished high school, and by the age of 23, I was hired as an officer with the Department of Corrections. In the academy, on the same grounds with police officers, we were trained to use the least amount of force necessary to apprehend a subject. However, on the streets, police officers follow these rules with everyone except black people.

In 1992, I was nominated by the administration to attend the National Association of Blacks in Criminal Justice being held in Phoenix that year. I was often called the nicest lady in DOC because I smiled a lot and got along with everyone. I accepted the invitation and gained a lot of knowledge and insight on many aspects of the African American experience in the criminal justice system and society. There was so much information to absorb; I had to obtain catalogs to purchase a lot of the material. I slowly built a library of African American literature, which includes titles such as, *Countering the Conspiracy to Destroy Black Boys*, *Empowering African American Males to Succeed*, *Hip Hop vs. Maat* and many other books that shed light on the conditions in our communities.

My road to activism started in 2016. A combination of past experiences and new information gave me a deeper insight into the causes of the African American struggle. The dots started connecting after I attended a play at the Tempe Center for the Arts. They broke down the song "Amazing Grace" and revealed that the author was a slave trader named John Newton. Several other scenes were thought-provoking. This was the same year the movie *Birth of a Nation* was released, and it shook me to the core. It was based on the autobiography of Nat Turner, the first black preacher. It showed how slaves were forced to be Christians and what happened to them if they did not comply.

Since that time, I have taken every opportunity I could to enlighten those who would listen. Although I am no expert on the subject of the African American experience, I am open-minded enough to research things about our history that I do not know. I share my vulnerable testimony to let others know that none of us are immune to police brutality and social injustice.

As the quiet and shy, young lady that everyone knew me to be, it was a total shock (even to myself) when I stepped out of character and made bold statements about our lack of consciousness and complacency to our status in society.

Trump was running for President, and many of us still did not feel the need to vote. We were programmed to just pray and trust God to solve all of our problems without contributing to the resolution process. We are currently in a race war (after the death of George Floyd), and black men and boys are still being murdered by police and hung from trees in 2020. The world is in an uproar right now, but activism is essential to overcoming this hurdle. It has become my mission (in the name of love) to help raise our expectations, improve our standards of living, and unite us as a people for the sake of future generations.

As an African American woman who was a teenage victim of police brutality, writing this article on love was a bit challenging during the height of a potential race war. As an introvert and empathetic person, reality no longer allows me to view life from the lens of religion.

As a retired employee from the Department of Corrections, with a desire to see all men and women treated fairly and equally, current events show that we have a long way to go.

If interested, I can be reached at kcooper36@outlook.com.

My Love
By Angelique Culver

It all began as Angelique, on her balcony in a white shirt and comfortable shorts, sat watching her love ready for the day she now knew would cause tremendous stress, and what could she do? Her part, she thought. Her hand pushed back her short, black, curly hair watching as the sun overtook the pink sky and welcomed the day. Angelique, 5'6" if she were standing, naturally, sun-kissed skin sat and wondered, what she could do to help her love?

The sky still retained a pink glow as the waves were crashing against the shore, calling to Angelique while she sits watching the love of her life work her magic, while the house and everyone in it were quiet. Unaware of what might be done before life begins anew as my love moves me into the tide of her new day.

Angelique observes the white sands on the empty shores as they spring to life. Her love tells her how hard it is to keep her sparkling sands pristine, the feel of silk being negated by boys in loud shorts, bleach blond hair, flip-flops, surfboards in tow leaving their careless tracks, littering the shoreline with toxic thoughts; immune to the damage done from their waterproof SPF 75. Head in the clouds, while she watches a family saunter by with their casual disdain for life.

Women in their Saturday best, beach towels trade secrets, pleasantries, make-up, nail polish living life behind a camera; stealing life from the family that understands her needs, knows that her coral dies with every self-involved Instagramer that arrives and tries to walk in solace with her leaving tiny footprints that give her nostalgia of days past, creating life not watching pictures of broken hearts tear hers away.

Theirs was a long-standing love. One that started when Angelique was just a child, fascinated by the waves she was happy to run right in. A part of that family leaving tiny footprints behind, she hoped anyway. Knowing though that she did not always do the right thing by her love, did not always know what the right thing was. She tried, she read up, and she tried. She was sure that failed, hurt, or angered her love, but she always came back and tried to do it right—tiny footsteps, nostalgia, making memories.

Angelique Culver, Esq., LLM, CHC is an attorney, she was named in the most influential Black attorneys in the country by Savoy Magazine 2018. Angelique graduated from Spelman College, Georgetown Law Center, and John Marshall Law School. She practiced as a public defender in Fulton County, Georgia. She was Chief Compliance Officer at Grady Hospital in addition to her job as a corporate attorney associate before the age of 30. She's on the executive management team for Vibra Healthcare as Chief Compliance and HIPPA Officer. She is a breast cancer survivor and current metastatic breast cancer warrior. Contact Angeliqueculver@bellsouth.net, or 404-934-4420.

Small Miracles
By Diana Culver

I was a preacher's kid at church at around eight years old. One of my father's parishioners asked how many kids I was going to have, and I replied six. Then she asked about a husband, and I explained that I do not need or want one.

Angelique, Miracle #1

I delivered the most perfect little girl ever. She was loving, adored, and precocious. She walked and talked early. A lady came to us and complimented Angel's (Angelique) pigtails. Angel at 18 months replied, "That's ridiculous, I have braids." She has a dynamic personality; she is gorgeous and was a mini-adult at three. When Angel was six, she announced that she was going to be a lawyer and was engaged. Angelique was public defender, in corporate law, in executive management, survived breast cancer, and is battling metastatic breast cancer. She is a badass, personally and professionally. Angel was named one of the top 100 most influential Black lawyers by Savoy magazine in 2018, my shero!

Ricky, Miracle #2

Ricky is and was stubborn even before he was born. Ricky is a big brain like his sister. He is and was so opinionated. At two, he informed me as we drove past Good Samaritan Hospital renovations; "Mama, when I grow up, I'm going to sell your apartments and buy an old hospital, tear it down, build a new hospital and charge sick people lots of money to come there." He is still running my life. He and miracle #3 have been in business with me for 20 years. He is in the honors college at Arizona State University (ASU), finishing another degree between managing my life, criticizing my parenting and business savvy.

Brocky, Miracle #3

What to give Ricky for his 2nd birthday? A little brother! This pregnancy was very difficult. I was admitted to the hospital 13 times for premature labor. He was born on December 2, 1983. Brocky was and is profoundly serious. Before kindergarten, he said, "Mama, I really prefer you send miracle #4 to kindergarten, I do not know those people that well." He is still that way. He has also been in business with me for 20 years. He is teaching and working on his masters at ASU. My uterus closed shop the day he was born. No more babies, right?

Brian, Miracle #4

I was not Brian's first Mama, that was red-headed Sharon. She was a friend. Near Brian's fourth birthday, Brian came to me permanently. Brian is and was a debater and argumentative. Coming from the church at four, he said, "When I grow up, I'm going to get me a big old house and a big old car. I am going to tell Jesus to give it to me!" Reverend Brocky (#3) said, "Jesus is going to tell you to get a big old job!" Brian has a job (with me for 20 years), a beautiful family, including his adored grandson, to argue with. But, wait there is more.

Patricia, Miracle #5

Brian came with a baby sister, Patricia. Patricia is hilarious. Her mission in life was to pester her brothers. Patricia loves her big sister, Angel. Angel cared for her when I went to work. Patricia has a baby fur-baby. She is now doting on the big sister who doted on her. She is her big sister's champion.

Geneva, Miracle #6

Geneva was Angel's best friend in 3rd grade. She had major challenges in her early childhood. She was bubbly, outgoing, loving, and personable. Geneva was the gift that kept on giving. She gave us five magnanimous darlings. She gifted the best of herself to her/our children. She showed up in court five times to tell the court that she wanted them with me. I see the best of her children in my youngest children daily!

Deija, Miracle #7

Deija saved my life. This bubbly, energetic little girl gave me purpose. She was again my mini-me too, and adored by her siblings. She was three and asked me, "Mama, you went to the nail store without me?" She is artistic, writes songs, sings, plays the guitar and keyboard. She is also Angel's baby. She is a senior at Kutztown.

Alaja, Miracle #8

Alaja was and is delightful. Her stature is small, and she was quiet around adults. At three, we went to Jamaica, reggae comes on, and she says, "Mama, that's Jamaica music!" She is a good student and daughter. She found her love and voice in competitive cheer. She is a girly girl. Alaja is a senior in high school and does not want to cheer this year. She wants to hang out and socialize instead. She is nearly grown (tears).

Alan, Miracle #9

Alan is a character. Like Brocky, he is serious. I was in the delivery room with him. In third grade, he asked his teacher during a shooter drill, "Well, what if he gets you?" The teacher was aghast and called me. He is brilliant with logistics and had devised a plan to keep the children safe even if the teacher was gone. He is like his sister, an incredible athlete. He played varsity quarterback in his freshman year. He has come into an identity crisis, trying to find his people. He is a sophomore at the time of the coronavirus. It's just not easy.

Kyle, Miracle #10

Kyle is like Brian. He loves to argue with everyone about everything. He was in second grade, and a girl got bit. We had a discussion, and I observed the class. Little bossy was seated next to my child. The teacher said to put pencils down. My child did not comply, but was finishing a sentence. Karen was out of her seat, in his face, "Teacher said pencil down," over and over. My kid ignored her. Little Bossy tried to yank the pencil from my kid (I wanted to bite her). I raised my hand, "Teacher, could you get bossy away from my kid?"

Love conquers all.

Diana Culver, M.Ed., Ph.D., has been the single mother of ten children for over 30 years. She is a mother first, an entrepreneur, advocate for her children and others. She is a self-proclaimed civil rights superhero (50-year activist) with a cape and love glasses. She is an educator of children, families, and the community. She is the author of *Real Families, Voice, Value, and Respect*, empowering parents and professionals to advocate for their children and those they serve. She has prior experience in corrections, sales, management, and with intellectually challenged people. Diana is a people builder. Contact: dculverphd@gmail.com or 520-560-5016

It's The Simple Things
By Linda Donegan

A wise man once said, "It's the simple things." This wise man was my dad, and that short, simple sentence is a gift that keeps on giving. I hope that by sharing some of my thoughts on how it's the simple things that matter most, I can pass this gift on to you too.

These words have guided me in my life, they have empowered me, healed me, inspired me, and changed me. Ironically it was Dad's wisdom that helped me to stay strong when he became ill and later in coping with the grief when he passed away.

It's fitting that I am writing this piece on Father's Day here in Ireland. Dad, this is my Father's Day gift to you. In Dad's later years, I could see that he was becoming disillusioned, saddened by all the news that was reported in the mainstream media. I know he was worried and, to reassure him, I would tell him stories about all the good people doing good things all over the world. It's a practice that I have kept up, always looking for the good, always shining a light on the good in the world, hoping to reassure others too.

Now look at us, Dad, we are in a book full of stories about the good in the world. Can you believe it? We are in a book together, Happy Father's Day Mr. Tom Donegan, now your gift to me is a gift for others too. Oh and give Aunty Pat a hug, I know she shares your appreciation for the simple things, so she'll enjoy this too.

Dad, you and I, we're going to do our little bit to remind everyone that it's the simple things in life that matter most.

My relationship with my dad taught me that gratitude and appreciation are powerful tools for healing and for experiencing joy even during the darkest of times. Throughout my life, hearing and saying the words "it's the simple things" has shaped me. I view the world through these words. It's the simple things that move me the most, from sunrises and sunsets to magical interactions with strangers. I notice the simple things.

In recent years I have become more and more interested in human connection and how simple things connect us. Have you experienced those moments with a stranger, when a simple smile, a hello, a chat can completely alter your day, warm your heart? There is something really special about authentic interactions with strangers. That gap between two people when filled with a smile, a 'hello' is not just seen by the eyes or heard by the ears, it is felt by the heart.

I'll tell you a little story.

A smile from a stranger, one simple smile through a foggy window in a coffee shop, a brief moment in time, a powerful moment that had so much meaning. I sat sipping coffee, alone, surrounded by people, tears streaming down my face as I observed life going on all around me. That day was three weeks after Dad had passed away, and I was struggling. I felt disconnected. People passing, chatting, talking on phones, laughing in groups, the chatter in the coffee shop, I felt so disconnected from it all. Then, the smile. The smile from a stranger, the brief moment of eye contact through the window. It was like time stopped, and I was pulled back from the abyss into a comforting hug—all that from a stranger's smile.

It only lasted a few seconds, the smile, the eye contact, but it was powerful, felt very deeply, and that feeling has stayed with me. I often wish I had run after my stranger and hugged him, he has no idea the impact his smile had on me. He went on about his day, completely unaware that he changed mine. He certainly doesn't know that I am writing about him in a book. I can't thank him, but I can thank you if you smile at strangers—thank you, you make a difference.

It makes you think, doesn't it? The impact that a simple gesture such as a smile can have. It's the simple things. It doesn't always take grand gestures, we don't need the solutions to help someone, we simply need to show we care or let someone know we see them. An authentic acknowledgement, be it through a smile, a hello, or a chat, is a way of saying, "You are not alone, you are not invisible, I see you." I know that because that's how I felt when my stranger smiled at me.

We are strangers to so many people, on any given day, especially if we live in an urban area we probably interact with more people we don't know than with people we do. Therein lies an opportunity. If we want to have a positive impact on the world around us, to create a kinder and more compassionate world, why don't we start with our interactions with strangers?

In today's world of separation and isolation due to Covid-19, in a world where leaders seek to divide us, where loneliness and depression are experienced by so many, it is becoming more and more important that we interact with love, kindness, and compassion. Together let's create a kinder, more loving, and compassionate world one interaction with a stranger at a time.

You may not be able to change the world, but you can alter how someone experiences living in it. Your smile reminds people that they are not alone, saying "hello" reminds people there is kindness in the world. Be the reason people believe there is good in the world. Kindness matters.

It's the simple things in life that are the most extraordinary.
~ Paulo Coehlo

Keep smiling xx

Linda Donegan is an energetic and passionate advocate for human connection and kindness. She is the founder of "Our KIND of World," an Irish grassroots movement powered by kindness, and an event coordinator with The Liberators International. Linda has coordinated global events that have brought thousands of people together to experience authentic kindness, human connection, unity, and joy in new and unique ways. You can email Linda at linda@theliberators.org.

I'm Gonna Love, Love, Love Until I Die
By Kate Doster

I learned about love through a pint-size, powerhouse package of glitter and cuss words. She showed me that true love is passionate, deliberate, rebellious, and diverse. Her name was Irene Soderberg, and she was a singer and performer. I met her on my birthday, shooting an event in L.A. Before the night was over, she was serenading me in front of dozens of people at the Hollywood Improv. She would continue to serenade me every year after on the phone. Irene was fearless and brave and the quintessential love rebel living with HIV. She was an advocate; she fell in love instantly with no predilection and loved you forever. This morning, I found out that my friend died, and I listened to her last voicemail to me. In the message, she relayed a song by Frank Sinatra called "I'm Gonna Live Till I Die" "I'm gonna live until I die, I'm gonna laugh 'stead of cry. I'm gonna use the town and turn it upside down, I'm gonna live, live, live until I die." As she spoke, her words ring true in my ears now, "Don't let your heart get hard, the world is still worth loving." Yes, it is darling girl, yes it is.

Kate Doster-Wright is a professional photographer and creator of the mentoring program, Send the Elevator Back for Me. Her goal as a photographer is to help you remove the mask that so carefully guards the polite smile to find the authentic you. Her passion is paying it forward in all aspects. You can reach Kate at kate@katedostermedia.com.

A Mother's Instinct: Love Grows & Blooms
By Rina Escalante

I have always felt light within my spirit, internal happiness that, as a child, I didn't know where it came from. I just wanted to share the warmth I felt within with others because if I felt good, wouldn't life be more pleasant if I shared that warmth? That light still shines brightly within my soul, and I've always felt compelled to share it.

Growing up in San Francisco in the early '70s was magical, the Summer of Love had just happened four years earlier. Our generation was witness to all types of love, we were able to play outside, and diversity was everywhere you looked. My little Catholic school in the Mission District was filled with love, warmth, and happiness! We were taught about Jesus' last commandment, "Love one another." To this day, I remember the simplicity of this concept, and the simple act of loving one another affected my entire being. Stewardship was how it was reinforced; giving of yourself became a natural act.

I'm the oldest sister of four siblings, and as long as I can remember, I was always told that I needed to set the example for my brother and sisters. I always felt a responsibility for how I behaved, so I tried to consciously do the right thing. Now, this is not to say I was perfect, far from it, my friends, as we all know this is a learning journey we are on after all. I was taught, and I believe that our almighty Creator is the only one who can claim perfection. I merely want to point out that my motherly instinct was instilled early on in life and possibly even before that.

When my siblings and I were young, I remember depending on my intuition to try to keep us out of trouble; however, I did not always listen to it. Since we were able to play outside, we would walk that fine line of playing and mischief, thinking about it now makes me snicker. I would trust my foresight to avoid getting into things or doing things that would give me that "feeling" in my stomach, that I have come to learn to be my solar plexus chakra. Throughout my life journey, what I have discovered is how on point my instincts have been. As my instincts progressed and time went on, wishing "if only I had listened every time the warning bells went off" were pointless because, without those life lessons, I would not have had experiences that helped me grow and develop as a mother, grandmother, woman, and, God-willing, one day as a Reiki healer and all the exceptional gifts that come along with it.

When I was a young mother, I used to read to my girls before they went to bed, for oh so many reasons. By the time each of them had turned five, I had done my best to prepare them for kindergarten by teaching them basics so they would not be lost on their first few days at school. I'm glad I listened and followed my instincts because in working with my daughters, I came to know their strengths and weaknesses, which made it easier for me to comm-unicate with their teachers regarding their educational needs.

I noticed that one of my girls, as sharp as she was outside of the classroom, was having challenges retaining information. I began to notice these challenges in her kindergarten year. Her teacher was very kind and supportive and asked me to wait another year before having any testing performed. So, I did wait, but there wasn't much improvement, and I was *feeling* that we were wasting valuable time by not testing her and getting her the support she needed. I knew how intelligent my daughter was and how logical her brain worked, which is why I was getting frustrated at their lack of urgency to get her the support she needed. But I *just knew* that she needed more foundational and fundamental support.

They were insistent that children that young are still developing at an elementary level. As far as I was concerned, they were wasting my daughter's valuable time. About six months into the school year of first grade, my instinct was banging loud and clear in my gut. I had to become insistent, and I went straight to the top and spoke to the administration of the school. I fought for my daughter. I secured the needed testing. They determined she had challenges in retention, among some other things, and she did get the extra support she needed! I met with her teachers, school counselors, and my daughter all the way through to high school. She made it, she graduated high school! I was so proud of her. *Follow your instincts, they won't steer you wrong.*

As life progressed, I continued to get messages from my instincts, most of the time, I followed their guidance, and other times I decidedly did not. When I did, I was always content with my decision. When I did not, I would usually beat myself up over it because I "knew better" than to not follow my own guidance. In an outburst, I would mutter, "I should have listened to my instinct!" However, as I look back, I must admit, I am grateful for those life lessons because through them is how we gain experience.

This next chapter in my life has allowed me to truly begin to bloom with all the gifts my Creator has given me. He has brought me to a very special group of women I call my "soul sisters." I adore them! I believe we need to be grateful for each moment and all the experiences we are brought through; they are life lessons. Don't think for one moment, anything that happens is *by accident.* Always believe a higher power is trying to elevate your life experience.

Look forward to those *life lessons*; they are meant to enhance our experience in some way.

Rina Escalante is a first-generation Salvadorian-American from the San Francisco Mission District.

She wholeheartedly believes that if you surround yourself with positive energy, you can make anything possible. She shares her life experiences in her storytelling with the intention that the reader will know they are not alone on their life journey; we all share common threads. Rina is currently studying the expansive world of Reiki and is currently working on becoming a Reiki Master with the love and support of her soul sisters. This is her third collaborative book. You can contact Rina at rinaesca@gmail.com.

The World's Manifesto
By Elvi Flores

August 11, First Day of School Eve, was a typically bright and beautiful El Paso Sunday. The next day would begin the 2019-2020 school year. Every teacher knows that this day comes with immense anticipation and countless questions. However, in 2019, the days before came with incredibly heart-wrenching questions. How would I help my 4th graders understand that a young man entered the Walmart five miles away from our school with the intent to shoot and kill as many Mexicans as he could? How could I explain something that I will never understand if asked? What words would I use to *prove* to them that the good outweighs the bad in our world every time?

Actually, I don't easily believe that it does. Although my life has been beyond blessed, I have seen and experienced enough to know that there is not always a happy ending. In fact, I lean more toward permanent pessimist than eternal optimist. My racing mind will seek out the worst-case scenario of any situation and play it perpetually. Fortunately, I grew up in an area of El Paso with a very racially diverse population close to Fort Bliss. Never having experienced a racist word or action against me, I now worried about the long-term mental impact of an armed white man targeting us because we are of Mexican descent. My students are nine years old. How would they see the world now? Would they avoid taking a risk out of the belief that they are hated by others? Would they hate in return?

This First Day of School Eve, I found myself parked at an empty Carl's Jr. parking lot. Not sure why there, there was numbness and disbelief around many of my actions in the days after the shooting. This time, my racing mind kept replaying a Facebook post written by one of my yoga teachers. To paraphrase, his post explained that we get to decide what we believe about the world as we step out of the house each day. If we believe we will encounter selfishness, then that is what we will notice. If we believe everyone is love, then we will see the love in everyone.

Guided by this powerful choice of how to see our world, I realized my students would need messages of support if I wanted them to choose to see love. The trauma and anxiety caused by the shooting would have an additional impact on their learning and general outlook of life. In the longer term, I wanted my students to believe they are just as valued and talented as anyone else from any race. In that Carl's Jr. parking lot, I nervously posted a request for messages of support on a closed educator Facebook group. The young man who killed 23 people on August 3rd had a *manifesto*. If I received a response, it would prove to my students that there is a love counterargument to his manifesto of hate.

The permanent pessimist in me believed we would receive enough messages to create a beautiful display, develop some pen pal relationships, and inspire some smiles. The world had a different plan, though. The Facebook response was immense and immediate. Teachers from all over the country requested more information and shared my post. I was amazed by how others were so impassioned and thrilled to support my students in my little classroom in El Paso.

By the third day of school, the first message arrived. It was a postcard written by a lovely grandmother in Las Cruces (a city in New Mexico about 45 miles away). The following day brought a beautiful letter and an autographed football from the Notre Dame football program. Part read, *Please accept this ball as a gesture of your efforts to exemplify the good in our world, and a reminder of faith in humanity.* (Me? These words leave a lump in my throat every time).

The following weeks brought mountains of boxes of mail to my classroom. We received tens of thousands of messages full of love and support from kids and adults from all over the United States. By the end of the month, people traveled to our school to offer their love and support as well. Companies like Love Glasses, LiveGlam, Stars of Hope and Raytheon came by to offer their support to our community. A wonderful family drove from Dallas with bags of stuffed animals for our students. There were beautiful messages from people of all ages. My students loved trying to decipher cursive handwriting used by elderly people reaching out to us from nursing homes all over the country.

People affected by recent mass shootings also reached out with powerful messages of hope. There were messages of love and strength from Las Vegas, Dayton, Midland, Santa Fe, Florida, and New Zealand, among others. A postcard from Dayton read: *We can consider each other brothers and sisters in tragedy. But I prefer to simply think of us as brothers and sisters.* Amazingly, the international response was just as huge. We received messages of love from Japan, Turkey, Spain, and all over South America, just to name a few.

One morning, my student, Liliana, twirled in delight when I told her she could keep a message from a student in Japan to add to the love scrapbook she had already created at home. Maybe hate and mass shootings are not something she thinks about often. I know kids are resilient that way. Even so, I am so grateful to all those who inspired her to twirl as a 9-year-old should.

As I write this, we continue to mourn the loss of our community members on that day. We will soon approach the first anniversary of that horrific day. Our hearts are still heavy, but the outpouring of love amazed and greatly supported our community. The world took time to remind us that we are loved, and for that, thank you.

My name is Elvi Flores. I'm a fourth-grade teacher in El Paso, Texas. I received my master's degree in Reading Education from the University of Texas at El Paso. In my 20 years of teaching experience, my favorite part of my job is seeing my students read, react, question, and play with ideas being presented by an author. My goal is to provide access to quality, thought-provoking literature to my students. Most of my free time is spent with the best dog in the world: my boxer, Ellie. My email is elviflores2@gmail.com.

The College Box
By Louisa Garrett

I knew this year was coming. It happens for all school-aged kids when they reach the end of their academic careers. Senior year. When she arrived at the start of her senior year of high school, things were already different. Nothing had changed, but everything was changing. Things were going to be different because that's the evolution of life. This was the last year I'd have with her. I mean, she would always be my Niece, obviously. My home would always be her home, obviously. But my heart explodes into a million pieces at the mere thought that where I live would no longer be where she lives. That is too much for my brain.

I cannot remember ever feeling like this before. I cannot remember ever feeling all the pieces of my heart trying to escape, but only rising up enough to clog my throat and make my eyes glisten.

Possibly when my father died, but I was only in the first grade. I remember coming back to school after the funeral. My mother had written a note for my teacher to explain my absence. Mrs. Douglas called me to her desk. She hugged me and asked if I was okay. My seven-year-old heart couldn't explain the depths of the pain. So, I said yes and then asked to go back to my desk. I sat down and stared at the math problems. As I finished my worksheet, I could feel the pencil marks crawl up my skin with each indentation. I get that same sensation now.

Possibly when I was nine and moved away from my friends to a strange new land. I could feel their eyes burning my skin as they focused on me when I entered the classroom. I get that same sensation now.

Possibly when my great-grandmother died. Grandmama was in her 90s, and I was a teenager. She had been sick for a while, in and out of the hospital. We made the two-hour car ride almost every Friday towards the end. I dreaded that drive. We had gotten back on Sunday. The phone rang early on Tuesday, two days after my 16th birthday. I already knew. I got up and started brushing my teeth. My mom came into the bathroom. This one hit me like a blunt object to the back of the head. I get that same sensation now.

When I think back to those heartbreaks, they feel a lot different than this, but the same too. The Niece will be leaving for college in a few short months. Simple as that. And there's nothing I can do to change it. So, what now? How do I stay excited for her as she makes big choices for her next life's adventures while I wade through the oceans of my emotions? Love.

I enter the house with a decent-sized cardboard box. Big enough to be filled with necessary life items. Big enough to distract me from the pieces of my heart floating through my body like sad confetti. This cardboard box is the answer to senior year. I am sure of it.

"What's with the box, Aunt Lou?" she asks as she sees me toss it behind the couch.

"This is your College Box," I exclaimed with my biggest smile, hoping she doesn't hear the cracks in my voice.

She looks at me with puzzlement as only a 17-year-old can waiting for more information. With my biggest smile still splayed across my face, I offer sweeping hand gestures as I explain to her that we will fill this box with all the things she will ever need for college.

"See. Your College Box," I say as I place a bottle of lotion in it and point like Vanna White. She smiles and shakes her head, yes. Then she goes to her room. Leaving me in the living room, staring at a huge box with one lone item inside. I stare at that box for hours crying crocodile tears. I want to kick it, but I don't. The College Box is symbolic, and it must be revered. I decided during those hours of waterfall eyes to fill the box with as much love as possible. The box is no longer just a container for things. It is an enchanted vessel of love.

Each time I go to the store, I purchase something for the College Box. The vessel gets filled with a variety of lotions and soaps and shampoos and conditioners and cleaning sprays and air fresheners and bleaches and deodorants and tubes of toothpaste and mouthwashes and laundry detergents and flosses and razors and feminine products. The Niece notices every item as the College Box fills up. She grabs an item or two at the store and looks at me and says, "College Box." I smile, and my heart breaks a little more. This is happening. She is leaving.

The days and weeks and months speed up. The College Box is completely full, and the time has come to drive her the 2.5 hours east. It's only 2.5 hours, I think. She will be practically down the street, I lie to myself. The pieces of my heart know she is leaving. The College Box knows it is leaving too. We pack the car.

"You got everything?" I say too excitedly.

"Yep, I think so," she responds.

"What if my roommate doesn't like me?" she asks.

"She will love you," I say emphatically.

We both smile and we both know I have no idea if this stranger will love The Niece. This stranger will surely not know that she has nightmares sometimes and that she needs hugs for reassurance.

The two cars with all of The Niece's belongings arrive at her new home. We unpack the cars. The College Box stares at me. It is time. I hug The Niece a little too long. I watch her walk to the room. I'm excited about her new adventures. The tears immediately start to flow once she's out of sight.

When I arrive at our house, I stare at her empty room for hours. There's stuff still in it, but the essence of her is gone. The College Box no longer sits in the living room as a constant reminder.

My phone vibrates.

"Thanks, Aunt Lou."

Louisa Garrett is the architect behind the movements #MakeKindLoud and Pass the Love, something that was born from her own frustration with the world, the politics, the negativity, the hatred towards others. Louisa examined her own story to discover things she didn't like and made a conscious decision to change the way she was showing up in the world. "Go be the change you wish to see in the world," that is what Louisa is doing. Now, she speaks to corporations, groups, organizations, schools, and challenges them to find ways to #MakeKindLoud.

She hosts weekly online conversations and interviews the heroes among us who are making the world better in their own kind ways. Contact: louisa@makekindloud.com.

Love And Justice For All
By Susie Gestrine

Love is a powerful and diverse thing. Most of us have a love for some people in our lives; our parents, our siblings, our partner, our children, our friends, and so on. There are many ways in which we show that love to the people around us. What if you have love in your heart for everyone? What can you do to express that love? These are questions I found myself asking back in 2011, a time when I found myself in a crossroads of my life. I saw so much hate and ugliness and injustice in the world, and I felt the need to play a small part in changing that for the better. That is when I began my journey into the realm of the political world and started volunteering with a political party. In this capacity, I was able to plan events for the community and bring people together for positive change.

After the election in 2016, we were all feeling pretty defeated. I sat with my horror and fears that everything we had worked so hard for was now going to fall apart and go away. That the country we love was going to revert to a darker time, and the battles for equality and justice we had won in recent years would be erased. However, after a little bit of time, I began to see people start to organize protest events and marches. People came together as I have never seen before with national events like the Women's March and many others. I was again wondering what I could do in these times, in my small community to help.

One day in April of 2017, I was skimming through my email and happened upon an email from MoveOn.org. They were planning a national wave of local events and calling it "Resistance Summer." They were only accepting a small number of people to become organizers and go through the training process to participate, I thought they would never pick someone from rural Arizona, one of the most conservative areas in the country. I decided to apply anyway, figuring I would never hear from them again.

About a week later, I got the news that they had chosen me to be an organizer! I went through the online training and learned so many valuable things about bringing people together for a unified cause. It was an amazing experience.

The first two events were smaller affairs to get out into the community and register voters and to learn how to canvass for petition signatures. The culminating event was to be a picnic to get people to come out and continue the conversation of how we could prevent some of the negative things that were coming out of the current political leadership. A way to motivate more people to show up and to volunteer to help get the word out for upcoming elections and other opportunities.

As I mentioned before, I lived in a small conservative town that, for the most part, supported the current events, and I was unsure if many people would even show up. I reached out to the handful of supporters I knew we had and publicized the event. I promoted the event online and even got it mentioned in the local newspaper. I was able to get a couple of speakers from the state level to make the four-hour drive from Phoenix to agree to attend. Now I was terrified, what if no one shows up? What if the people that opposed us showed up to cause trouble like they had threatened to do online? Was this going to be a huge disaster and a letdown?

That hot July Saturday morning, I loaded up my car with food and games and decorations and drove up to the park. The couple of people that volunteered to help set up came, and we got everything ready for a typical summer barbecue. We had giant lawn games and inflatable boxing gloves, we had bubbles and balloons, we had hot dogs and potato salad. Everything was ready. I was getting nervous because I heard the speakers were running late and no one was there yet. Then a car pulled in. Then another one, and another one. People kept coming. They were excited to find other like-minded individuals in a community that they thought they were alone in. The speakers arrived and pumped up the crowd, people ate and talked and enjoyed themselves. Relationships and friendships grew that day, and many of the people that came to that picnic went on to become invaluable volunteers to continue doing the work that needed to be done to change things for the better. No one came to disrupt our gathering or cause any problems. I was amazed at the success of this event that I had organized.

I learned that day that when you do things with love in your heart, good things come of it. No matter how small or insignificant you think that your actions might be, they will lead to bigger, greater things over time. Every single person has something they can contribute to the bigger picture.

My fight for social justice and change continues and will continue for the rest of my life. I will never stop trying to create a better world for all of us and hope one day there is nothing left to fight for. In the words of the great Justice Ruth Bader Ginsberg, "Fight for the things you care about, but do it in a way that will lead people to join you." I believe that way is through love. Love for yourself, love for your friends, love for your community, and love for the world. Love always wins.

Susie Gestrine is a political organizer and activist for social justice. She strives to be a positive role model in her community and to assist others in having their voices heard, either through voting or organizing community events. Her passion is spreading love far and wide to all who seek it! You can reach Susie at Susannah.Gestrine@gmail.com.

Discovering Self-Love
By Patricia Holgate Haney

In everyone's life, at some time, our inner fire goes out. It is then burst into a flame by an encounter with another human being. We should all be thankful for those people who rekindle the inner spirit. —Albert Schweitzer

I was at a place in my journey where I was between looking back and looking forward—the mid-way point in your life where your past is further away than your future.

My journey had a lot of bumps in the road, really some were like trenches, but I had made it through with a few road burns and some great fun along the way.

I had finally found true love and relationship peace and had been blessed with two great sons; I had a set of fantastic parents who I was remarkably close to who embodied love and a supportive family.

I had an eclectic circle of friends, and I traveled a lot, which had always been a dream and passion. My sons had made lives for themselves and had families of their own and were establishing their new traditions. I didn't feel needed any longer. I realized that was a good thing. My goal was to raise boys to become men who treated their partners with respect and love, who were confident but also sensitive and not afraid to show it. That goal had been accomplished. Overall, I was extremely fortunate.

But I still felt like I had not done enough, been good enough or accomplished enough. It was a cloud that hung over me, some days worse than others. For some reason, I could feel joy for others, but not for myself.

About a year ago, just another typical morning, it began with me already feeling overwhelmed. All I saw were things to be done, how bad I felt I looked, and how much I hadn't done and still had to do. Feeling frustrated, I got my things together and left for work and to match my mood, it was a strangely cold and gray day for Arizona.

I was listening to the news on the radio, even though it made me angry to listen, I still wanted to feel informed. I heard the usual rhetoric and wondered if we would ever get out of this mess before it was too late. Families and friends were being splintered by the division that was coming down from the top. Since 2016, conversations had gone downhill, and there seemed to be no middle ground, no trying to understand. Frankly, the mood of the country matched what I was feeling internally, and it was exhausting.

The wind was blowing dirt and debris into the air when I arrived at the intersection.

Standing in the middle of this whirlwind of debris was a young woman in a short-sleeved shirt wearing flip-flops. She was holding a baby wrapped in what looked like a thick, cozy blanket wearing a little knit cap. She hugged the baby to her chest. I couldn't help but think how cold she must be.

The light changed, and in my rearview mirror, I saw her carefully cross the street to a bus stop. I wondered who she was. Where was she going? Did she have anyone to take care of her?

It all fell into place for me—the proverbial light bulb moment. The timing was right, and my mindset changed that day. I had let the negative thoughts I harbored cloud the reality of what I did have. I didn't have to be perfect. I was good enough. I also had the ability to channel my energy and resources into action. I had something to give. This young woman helped me see things clearer than I had for a long, long time. I realized I was grateful for what I had. I was loved, even though I couldn't love myself.

In my dark times, I had the help of family, friends, and faith. I had hands reach out to help me up. How could I have forgotten what that meant and felt like? For some, the darkness never goes away, and the future looks like it holds no hope. I had light, I had hope, and I had love. I had to start with loving myself and accept the imperfections. I decided at once to practice living with gratitude, an open heart, and to act.

Being a news junkie, I had become aware of the growing number of homeless and had begun educating myself on mental health issues that were being ignored or still had stigmas attached. Historically, the homeless populations were mostly in urban areas. The lack of mental health care, the economy, the raging pandemic, and current political crises were all contributing to the astronomical increase in the homeless population, and it was evident everywhere.

By acknowledging what I had to be grateful for and by loving myself, I found I had love to give. I began volunteering, finding organizations and people who were trying to implement change and give hope. I realized I could help make a change: one action, one person at a time.

Today when I start my day, I feel grateful for the love in my life, I feel that it is not wrong to love yourself. It took me a long, crazy journey to get here, but the love in my life multiplies every day. Giving love, I was blessed with new love.

Loving yourself is empowering. Giving love is life-changing. Love is expressed in countless ways, and no matter who you are, you have love to give. Realize each action makes a difference. Love is a never-ending circle that brings us all together.

The greatness of a man is not in how much wealth he acquires, but in his integrity and his ability to affect those around him positively. —Bob Marley

Patricia Holgate Haney is a travel professional following a career in management in both the for-profit and non-profit sectors. She volunteers for organizations dedicated to working with the underserved and unrepresented. An avid traveler, she enjoys meaningful discourse and exploring self-improvement.
Reach her at pholgatehaney@gmail.com or at LinkedIn.

Love Is Everywhere
By Marianne Hudspeth

There are so many ways that love can manifest, that I could fill a book, not just a chapter in this book. But for me, finding love took a long, long time.

I learned to find love after decades of feeling unloved. I was born in a small town in Iowa, and things seemed pretty normal until I was six years old. That's when things fell apart. It was a bright, sun-warmed day in April when I was playing outside in the driveway, happy to finally be able to be out after the long Iowa winter.

As my dad drove slowly down the gravel lane, I was so happy to see him, not knowing he was bearing devastating news that would change my life. As he got out of the car, he knelt down to my eye level.

He was quiet to a few seconds.

"Mommy is going to die," he said.

I remembered that she had been in the hospital for a few days. I thought there must be some mistake.

I said, "No, Daddy. She will be okay. The doctor is taking good care of her."

Then, he started to sob, and he looked in my eyes and said, "Mommy died late last night."

I was in shock and terribly sad and felt untethered. I had so many questions. Who will love us and take care of us? Who will pick me up when I cry? Did she die because of all the bad things I had done? Or thought? Was it because I was not kind enough to my brother?

My mother's death was caused by kidney disease at age 27. That loss left my father devastated. I know that he felt completely overwhelmed with my brother, who was only two years old and me, only six. He had no idea how to deal with this situation, and he self-medicated with alcohol, for many years. My brother and I didn't see much of him. He lost his job.

His parents very reluctantly and resentfully moved in with us. My grandparents felt stuck with us and told everyone the same. It was a lonely life on the farm where we were clearly a burden. I always felt 'less than.' Never enough. Certainly not loved.

But we always had a dog that loved me. When I was lonely, I would frequently talk things out with Tiny. One day out on the porch, I was talking to Tiny about missing my mom and how I felt around other kids talking about their moms. I didn't know anyone was listening. Tiny was wagging and giving me kisses when I heard that gruff voice of my uncle George, who was inside the house but heard me talking to Tiny through the screen door. Clearly, he was angry and scolded me, saying, "Why would YOU have reason to complain? You're just selfish! You're so lucky that someone is taking care of you and giving you food and a place to live! I don't ever want to hear you complaining again!"

Then I spent a large part of my growing years NOT complaining and secretly searched for a "Mom" that didn't think I was selfish and disgusting. My mom had two sisters,

Mary (Mame) and Dorothy (Sister). They were very nice to me, but I wasn't allowed (by my grandparents) to visit them often. Mame even asked my dad if she and her husband could legally adopt my brother and I. That just made him angry and offended even though he was an absentee dad. He did not want us to become "spoiled rotten."

But dogs never rejected me. The dogs always loved me. I was enough for them.

My husband, Jim, and I have been married for 25 years in December. He is my beloved and most days he (says) he likes me just fine. He loves me as much as any dog I've ever had. I do things well enough for him, and he makes me feel loved. As a bonus, he loves dogs too.

Jim and I found a special dog named Bailey. We named her because she was the same color of Baileys Irish Cream, a favorite beverage. We chose her because even though she had just met us, she loved us more than food. There, in the middle of all this puppy love, I noticed that while all of the pups were playful and wrestling when the breeder put a bowl of food down, all of those pups ran to the food dish, except one. Bailey sat still in front of me, just wagging her tail. She was actually smiling. She wanted to hang with us more than she wanted food! How in the world could we walk away from that kind of love? We had to take all of that puppy love home with us.

I have a great friend, Cynthia, who at that time did the testing for ATD, the therapy dog organization. She met Bailey and said, "She would be a great therapy dog! Let's test her. She has a great temperament." So, Cynthia tested

Bailey and me, and that's how we became a therapy team. We visited people who were lonely or were unable to get out on their own, like hospice patients. We would go see them at patient facilities or in their home or hospitals or wherever they were. Bailey loved her therapy visits and was so excited every time she saw her therapy dog vest, she would *run* to the car and patiently wait for the hatch to open. That's not true. She was not patiently waiting for me. She was ecstatic to go to work.

Bailey, at 135 pounds, was a little scary looking to some people, but sometimes being big is a good thing! I remember one time when we were visiting a dementia unit in a skilled nursing facility. One of the residents (I'll call her Lily) was sitting in her wheelchair just kind of staring into space. As Bailey and I entered her sight, she became quite animated and shouted, "My Pony Boy, My Pony Boy! I have been looking for you all day long! I'm so glad you're here! We thought you were lost! I love you, my Pony Boy." Her nurse, tearfully shocked and amazed, said that Lily had been nonverbal for three years. Bailey leaned into her, giving her kisses and wagging her tail, so happy to be Lily's pony that day.

That day, Bailey and I were enough. That day we got so much more love than we gave.

Then one day, Bailey was just not her happy self. She didn't dance with joy when she saw her therapy dog vest. She was not hungry, not thirsty, didn't want to go outside. She didn't run to the car when I opened the hatch. She panted harder than usual. She was probably in pain. She even looked sad. I knew something wasn't *okay*. I called her vet and took her for a visit. He ran some blood work and took x-rays. She was dehydrated and anemic. The doctor gave her an IV. He said to bring her back tomorrow, and we will see how she is. We brought her home and helped her out of the back of the car. She laid down and clearly didn't want to get up again. I asked her to please come, and she wobbled to her feet and went straight to her bed. Jim and I laid down beside her for a while and told her what a good girl she has always been. We told her how much we had always loved her, and that love was forever. We would take back to the doctor in the morning and gave her many hugs and kisses. We told her if she needed to cross the Rainbow Bridge, we would see meet her later. I know that she understood us.

After a while, we left her to rest, and we went to bed. Jim woke up at 3:00 a.m., and he went to check on her. He touched her gently, and she turned to look at him and took her last breath. Now, her ashes stay in the cedar box in the living room, but her love stays in my heart.

We found another Mastiff breeder and got a pup and named her Bailey's Coda Feels Like Love. In musical terms, Coda means a more or less independent passage, at the end of a composition, introduced to bring it to a satisfactory close. The love continues.

Marianne is a published author, naturopathic physician, registered nurse, Reiki Master, observer/tester for ATD (therapy dogs), and has organized several medical mission trips to Haiti to deliver healthcare. Her passions include being a helper in the world and a lover of justice and peace. She rides her own H-D Sportster Touring motorcycle and loves spreading love through humor. She is a self-proclaimed badass.

She lives in Arizona with her beloved and retired (God help her) husband, Jim.

She can be reached at Jimariahup@aol.com or 623-206-4017.

Growing More Than Veggies
By Martin Hutchison

I believe that the local church is called to be an agent of God's blessing and love in the world, with no strings attached. So, for 25 years, as a pastor, I was constantly pushing the church out of the building into the community. In 2015, I was exhausted, weary from pushing the church to be outward focused with limited success. I was ready to quit the ministry and do something else. Then I attended a meeting where our city council president suggested the possibility of using vacant city lots to create community gardens. I left that meeting, knowing where I wanted to make that happen and determined to help my congregation do so as a way to bless and love our neighbors.

For years, the church I pastor has worked cooperatively with three other very diverse churches to host a homeless men's shelter for two weeks every winter. At my encouragement, we held a joint meeting of folks from all four churches. We discussed the idea of a community garden. We formed a team to further explore the idea. A second idea that had a great deal of interest involved hosting a summer feeding program for students, which would eventually become included in our work in the garden.

After working with the city council for many months, we reached an agreement to lease a vacant, trash-strewn, dog-poop-laden lot from the city for $1 a year. We raised funds to build 20 raised garden beds, 24 feet long by 4 feet wide. A team from the church built the garden beds, and our youth helped place them on the lot. A friend who had a Bobcat loader offered to move the six dump truck loads of soil into the 20 beds, a task that could have been done in a couple hours. But I refused his help because I felt we needed the bonding experience, as a community, of hand shoveling the soil into the beds. We announced the workdays and neighbors came, parents and children from the nearby elementary school came, church members from all four churches came, community members came, city council members came, television crews and newspaper reporters came. In three weekends, we had all the garden beds filled with soil, seeds planted, and the community more connected.

The garden is located adjacent to a playground, and it was our hope that we could engage children in the task of nurturing seeds, learning where food comes from, and enjoying fresh organically grown veggies. The first night we were there, six neighborhood children, who were playing on the playground, came over to investigate what we were doing and were eager to help. As the work to establish the garden continued, more and more children became curious and excited to join in the experience. Imagine the smiles when the seeds they planted grew into plants and then veggies that they could harvest to share with their families for free.

It wasn't all smooth sailing. As summer progressed, those same children became bored. The boredom led them to enjoy throwing veggies. We didn't get upset, but we saw this as an opportunity to teach them about the value of food. We hosted field trips from their school, where they learned about gardening. We brought in a chef to turn veggies into something they would eat. The second summer, we partnered with the board of education and hosted the Summer Lunch in the Garden. The children enjoy lunch, develop relationships, play games, create art, do crafts, and spend time with adults who affirm and value them. The incidences of veggie mischief decreased, and the number of engaged children increased as meaningful relationships developed.

A local Rotary Club funds an annual Art program, which has become a highlight of the children at Summer Lunch in the Garden. Local non-profits and businesses partner with us to teach health classes, read books, mentor students and develop relationships.

We noticed that neighbors from the big houses up the street and neighbors from the apartments nearby were coming to the garden and becoming more connected. We saw people from varied economic levels working side by side. The police chief told us that what was once a high crime neighborhood saw a drastic reduction in crime. She attributed this to the garden's positive impact in the neighborhood. The story of the garden's transforming impact has been widely shared through local media and a variety of other outlets. As a result, we have seen an increase in interest in community gardening in both our city and in nearby towns.

As I worked in the garden with neighbors the first year, I noticed a boarded-up brick home that was in disrepair and an eyesore in the community. I suggested to our mayor that the home could serve as a much-needed community center for our children. With minimal encouragement, the city not only bought the home at a foreclosure, but the city has invested well over $250,000 in renovating it. It will soon be opened as a community center for the children and families of the neighborhood. A 3,780 square foot home has been given a new life and will enhance the life of the neighbor-hood.

Seeds of love can be small, but their impact is huge. Sowing seeds of love has changed our city one vacant lot at a time. It has changed the lives of community children, turned neighbors into friends, and redefined the mission of several churches in our community. And it has changed my life immensely.

"Growing More than Veggies" isn't just our tagline, it is what we do at the Camden Community Garden in Salisbury, Maryland.

Pastor Martin Hutchison has been the pastor at Community of Joy Church in Salisbury, Maryland since 1999. He is the founder of the Camden Community Garden and is the city of Salisbury's Secretary of Community Gardens. He serves as one of the founding Commissioners of the city's Kindness Commission. He has been married 32 years to Sharon, and they have two grown daughters.

Her Love
By Mindy Renee Jaffar

The faded superhero bed sheets were beaded up and smelled stale. The room was dark, but there was a hint of light seeping through the cracked door. The head of the old oak bunkbed nearly touched the doorframe, and every shadow gave me hope that it was my mom there to get me. I was told I could sleep on the top bunk until she came to pick me up, but sleep was not my priority, staying awake was. Besides, I barely knew these people, and I think the mattress might have been peed on. I compulsively shifted from my left to right side, trying to tilt my head so I could keep my eyes on the light, certain she would be there soon. It was my weekend with her, and surely, she wanted to spend every minute with me, or at least most of her time within the next 48 hours.

"Baby—wake up. I'm here, it's time to go," my mom whispered as she stroked my soft brown hair out of my eyes. I squinted at her, wondering how I neglected my duty of hallway light watching. Then I focused on her and was relieved that she was there for me. I smiled and sat up, reaching out for her to pull me off the bed. I was only five years old and still light enough for her to hold me for a moment. She rescued me from that unfamiliar space and held me tight. I laid my head on her shoulder and could hear the saliva maneuver behind her large and glorious smile, and I was happy.

"Who loves you, baby," she asked.

"You do!" I replied.

The smell of her cheap perfume-laced rabbit fur coat and remnants of her last Crown Royal on the rocks were a joyous notification that she was there with me. Never mind that she was boozed-up and chose to send me to a babysitter while she partied on "her" weekend. She was there now, and I wanted her, drunk or sober. I just wanted to be with her.

That wasn't the only night in my childhood where I laid somewhere, I shouldn't have been, but it's one that sticks with me. A night I felt abandoned, alone, desperately wishing my life was normal and that my mom was like the other moms—home, cooking, reading bedtime stories, and most of all, one who would never leave me.

As I grew older, nights like these were accompanied by increased anger. On numerous occasions, I beseeched her not to leave me, threatening to take back my love for her. But a grudge was never something I could hold on to, especially with my beloved mother. I often wondered what kept me hopeful and completely devoted to her, and the answer is quite simple—it was love.

Yes, love. On numerous occasions, I wondered if she would go out even though I was visiting her. Many nights, I lay watching the clock and watching one child after another leave. At the same time, I stayed behind until the morning light. During the days, I lay next to her while she stayed in bed, recovering from her long night, just to bring her an orange popsicle and her cigarettes. I wouldn't leave her side. But never once did I doubt if she loved me. Not one second of one day of one year; I knew she loved me. I knew by the warmth of her hug, by the joy written across her heart when she saw me, and by the humble apologies she frequently offered. Still, mostly her love was apparent because she told me so.

I know words can be like old cardboard boxes, empty and useless, but they can also be a box full of wonderful gifts like love and adoration. We hear countless songs and poems that dispute the impact of words, but I find solace in those string of letters. Tell me you love me, I'll believe you. Tell me you'll come back for me, I'll be waiting. And tell me I'm beautiful, I will smile and stand a little taller. You see, during my younger years, her words were what I had to cling to. Like an "oh shit" handle in the passenger seat, I held on tight to how she expressed her love because the alternate reality would've killed me.

Eventually, I let go of that handle, and everything leveled out. My mom moved across the country from Alaska to Texas and finally settled in Washington. She let go of the poison that nearly took her down and spent the rest of her life reconciling the pain she caused. The beauty was that it was already reconciled every time she appeared. Loneliness and forgiveness co-existed because she loved me, and I loved her. I loved her pork chops and mashed potatoes, I loved how she'd run my bath and sit on the edge, talking and laughing with me. I loved how she would kneel down in front of the toilet to rub my chubby little belly while I complained that I had to poo-poo. But what I loved most was her honesty. Through her tears of regret and obnoxious laughter, she showed me her love.

She wasn't a bad mom; she was an 18-year-old run-away who had spent the last few years looking for love herself.

The frigid Anchorage streets pushed her into the deceptive tacky bars, and she numbed the pain of losing me as well as the lies that plagued her mind that she wasn't good enough to be a mom. She taught me that love is honest and warm. She taught me to forgive and did exactly what the revered Maya Angelou advised, "When you know better, you do better. Forgive yourself."

She always came back, she always told me she loved me, and she always showed me who she really was, good and bad. She was love, and I embodied where she left off. Because of her, I am love too.

Mindy Renee Jaffar is a retired Navy Chief Petty Officer from Anchorage, Alaska. She has a BS in Healthcare Management, a MA in HR Development, and is currently working on a second Masters in Narrative Studies. She writes periodically on her blog, Dear Mindy and is near completing her first book, "She Had a Name"; a true crime memoir detailing the events of her mothers murder and how restoration is possible if we choose to attain it. She is dedicated to sharing women's stories of tragedy and resilience.

Keep Living
By Uzma Jafri

Whenever I met someone *really* old as a child, as in anyone over 25, they would lay their right hand on my head. "Keep living," they said.

I thought this was a silly Urdu blessing because what else was I supposed to do? I didn't do anything dangerous enough to die at six years old unless I counted the time I stuck my finger in an anthill. I dutifully bowed my head and lifted my cupped right hand to my face in *aadaab*, receiving the blessing. As a second-generation kid, I did what I was taught.

The laying of right hands by my Indian-Pakistani community was thus a different ordination or healing—a preventive measure to ward *away* spirits rather than encourage them to enter me. Always on the head, always, "Keep living." Sometimes it was accompanied by other blessings:

"May you have a tall husband and righteous children."

I was 12 and had had a growth spurt. The potential catastrophe of marrying a short man was averted in this way.

"May you be a credit to your parents."

I was 14, already knew everything, and my parents worried about my mouth. I don't know if this blessing manifested, because I still stick my foot in my mouth.

"Keep living. Stay happy."

I hear it to this day and never tire of it. It definitely works.

Religious people admonished me for bowing to receive the blessing. A cupped right hand to the face with head bowed, or *aadaab*, was a gesture created by Indians under Muslim rule. The standard Islamic greeting in Muslim India was replaced with a non-sectarian *aadaab*, so that non-Muslim subordinates could be acknowledged by their rulers. However, in Islam, there are no superiors or subordinates, and bowing to anyone other than God is considered idolatry.

God knew I worshipped Him alone, so I continued to bow my head before my elders, only to receive a blessing, not to worship them. If they weren't going to be stingy with their love, I wasn't going to withhold mine. We were not a community that said, "I love you," to each other, nor were we huggers outside of holidays, weddings, or funerals. The best I could expect was to be told, "Keep living," because that meant someone still wanted me around. That's what love looked like. The only way I could reciprocate was to get straight A's, never date, clean my plate, and execute a perfect *aadaab* when I was blessed.

My grandfather Nanajan was not a talker or a hugger. An abusive, motherless childhood and the British military fashioned his impeccable work ethic, perfect posture, slicked hair just longer than a crew cut, and utensils to eat Indian-Pakistani food, which is eaten by hand. On the phone, he provided a hurried report on how fine he was and closed with, "Okay, keep living." I imagine his hug was the same as Herman Munster's, Nanajan's doppelganger minus the bolts in his head. It was stiff and formal, like hugging a redwood. But his right palm opened wide to put on my head, never cheap with his blessing, "Keep living." Short, sweet, and loving.

At some point, his hands couldn't manage his meticulous grooming regimen anymore, and he needed help taking medication. He moved to a nursing home, his tall back ramrod straight in a wheelchair. When he stopped sitting up, eating, and became confused, he moved to a hospice unit. A temporary feeding tube was placed through his nose to prevent weight loss. With a history of sinus issues, the tube was a great offense and irritation, one Nanajan continually tried to remove. Restraints in nursing homes were allowed then, so soft ties kept his wrists tethered to the bed. Now unable to blow his nose, he was forced to mouth breathe, a thick cake of saliva and slime coating his tongue green-black.

I was visiting, and my task was to loosen the soft ties just enough so that he couldn't reach up and yank the tube out. On my first night, I addressed his oral care. At 93, he had his own teeth from a lifetime of obsessive brushing and flossing. The damp swabs from hospice helped me work the cake off his tongue. He was thirsty, sucking the water off the swabs. We sat face to face as I worked on his mouth and his thirst.

The next night, it took nearly an hour because I used one swab to hydrate him, several others to clean his mouth, tongue, and palate. We created a rhythm, and he was cooperating, knowing when to suck and when to be still so I could clean out his mouth. I talked to him, and he seemed to understand but didn't say a word. The restraints were slack and forgotten, so as his left forearm rose, I forced it down with my elbow gently, both my hands engaged in his oral care. This went on several times until I protested, "Nanajan!" I was exasperated, sleep-deprived, and leaving the next day. To study. To be a physician. To be fine. To keep living when I knew he wasn't. I continued my task when his left forearm fell hard on my right shoulder. I protested again in pain, but he heaved his left hand on the side of my ear, then on top of my head.

My stunned eyes locked with his glistening ones, and I experienced *knowing*. At that moment, with the dead weight of his left hand on my head, I bowed mine, overwhelmed with the heaviness of love. While he tried freeing himself all night to give me what he had left, I kept restraining him. "Keep living." In silence, he gave, and I received a last blessing. As his hand slid to my shoulder again, I cried my apology into it before it fell limp on the bed. I untied his wrists and threw away the restraints. He fell asleep and never fought the feeding tube that night.

Weeks later, I returned for the funeral and sat in a car as men carried Nanajan to a snowy grave. He was laid to rest next to my grandmother, his hands neatly folded right over left on his chest. Free.

"Keep living," they said.

Uzma Jafri is a mom of four kids and a physician in private geriatric practice. Her work includes medical direction advancing elder care and teaching future physicians. She is passionate about empowering Muslim moms to face their fears and challenges with humor and courage. To that end, she cohosts, "Mommying While Muslim," which addresses the unique challenges of second-generation Muslim Americans raising their children in post 9/11 America.

It can be found on all podcast platforms and @mommyingwhilemuslimpodcast on Instagram.
Email Uzma at uzma@mommyingwhilemuslim.com.

Love In Action
By Michon Javelosa

To me, love is acting on the core values which are at the center of our hearts.

It was in my DNA. My mom, a director in the Peace Corps, my dad, a political activist who was incarcerated in his native Philippines for sedition and inciting rebellion during the dictatorship of Ferdinand Marcos.

I grew up watching my mother volunteer at the Women's Shelter and Arlington Handicapped Association in Texas and work tirelessly for Kids Voting in Arizona. Both parents labored to cultivate a community that values diversity and inclusion in Michigan while volunteering for political campaigns to make sure their voices were heard regarding policies and issues in our country at large.

The central message to me was, "Be involved! It is our duty." In this context, my core values were set. The expression of love comes through action upon these values.

When I was about six, I remember lying on the carpet in our Ft. Worth home pouring through a collection of children's magazines, a treasure trove of Ranger Rick's, Zoobooks, and Highlights. I had recently read about habitat destruction and endangered and extinct animals, and I wanted to find out everything I could to help the affected animals. In doing so, I discovered that the depletion of the ozone layer was only making things worse.

I was outraged as I read that stopping ozone layer depletion could be achieved if more people became aware of the harm and were inspired to act. I was convinced that sharing this information would stir in others that same love for the Earth that I had, and they would immediately change anything they were doing that was contributing to the destruction. Hence the first of my soapbox tirades was born.

"Mom! Dad! Did you know that if people would stop using hairspray, leaving their refrigerator doors open, and using Styrofoam, that we could help save the Earth?! We need to tell people!"

"What are you going to do about it?"

"We need to get this article out to everyone. Then they'll know and change what they're doing! Dad, will you copy these pages for me? I need enough for everyone in our neighborhood."

I remember sitting where I'd had my ozone layer a-ha moment, diligently collating the pages into neat little packages, carefully stapling the top left corners so that people would understand that this was important infor-mation. Upon completion, I loaded them into my Muppets on Ice canvas satchel. I jumped on my banana seat bike with the dorky tall orange flag attached to the back. I was ready to distribute while my parents supervised from the driveway overseeing my door to door endeavor.

As I raced up the walk to the first house, I just *knew* if people understood the dangers of CFCs (Chloral Floral Carbons), they would start a chain reaction impacting the world and saving the ozone layer. Mr. Burton opened the door and said he wasn't interested in whatever gift wrap or candy bars I was selling.

Once it was clear I had no items to sell, he (and subsequently our other neighbors) listened politely for a few minutes, then cut me off and took the papers so I'd go away and let them resume their lives. This was the first time I realized that simply presenting information would not stir people into acting. I was heartbroken.

But this disappointment did not stop me. Throughout my childhood and young adult years, my love in action manifested itself in a multitude of ways. I always had a yearning to do more, a feeling that my love wasn't being expressed "enough."

I organized fellow students to convince our elementary school to start a recycling program and stop using Styrofoam trays (a win for the ozone layer!). I became a vegetarian in third grade because of my love for animals. I helped form a Cultural Unity Club in my high school to promote acceptance and diversity in Sturgis. And as a college student, I volunteered with a non-profit arts organization to bring artistic expression as a means of healing to children in underserved communities.

In 2013, Typhoon Haiyan struck the Philippines causing vast devastation. Infusions of funds from around the world were sent to aid the islands. Still, because of corrupt government practices, many funds were not distributed where needed. Inspired by Mahatma Gandhi's quote, "Be the change that you wish to see in the world," I founded a non-profit called Be the Change United and connected with a trusted partner in the Philippines. We were able to identify Giporlos, a town that needed a school building that could also serve as a safe evacuation center in times of crisis.

With the need identified, the fundraising began. I launched an online campaign using email and Facebook, worked with a local jewelry maker who created necklaces and donated the profits, and traveled to Houston for an in-home fundraising dinner. The intense efforts paid off. Be the Change United raised $20,000, and the school/emergency shelter opened on September 18, 2015.

I thought launching the non-profit and doing something that seemed big would make me feel like I was doing that elusive "enough." It didn't. What I have learned is that making change is important, but the action does not have to be big. There's not some trophy to be won or a finish line to cross. When you are called to act through love, it is an everyday process tapping into whatever is stirring inside you that needs to be made tangible.

This stirring is different for each of us. For me right now, it is working hard to raise my children to leave this world better than they found it, being Vegan, speaking out and marching for justice and equality, and taking time for self-care.

I encourage you to listen to your stirrings and explore what you can do to turn your feelings into action.
What do you love, and how will you act on it today?

Michon Javelosa is a serial entrepreneur who wants to live in a world filled with empathy, equality, and an abundance of vegan treats. A current expression of her love in action is spreading awareness on how to live a lifestyle rooted in compassion by using a platform she co-founded. You can reach Michon and find out all about it here: vKind.com.

The Magical Power Of Love
By Sharyn Jordan

In the magical summer of 1969, serendipitously, I met the most beautiful young man named Jay. Our magical love was at first sight. After a few months, and both never even desiring to marry, each of us at the tender age of 21, were over the moon to become married. It was evident we had found our twin flame, basking in the radiant glow of love's magic. As co-manifestors, my beloved Jay and I created a life of beauty, joy, and abundance.

After several months of marriage, we moved from our home state of Texas to Los Angeles, where my brother was a budding art student. He introduced us to his Hollywood friends, a profound I Ching scholar, and to an enigmatic art world. The social upheaval was in full glory. Therefore, it was an honor to participate in passion projects, such as a movement to remove lead from gas and eventually preventing the smog of air toxicity, being on the pilot Earth Day committee, and attending movie premieres at the then-historic Grauman's Chinese Theatre was incredible. Visiting Disneyland every weekend, seeing Elton John at the Troubadour on his first breakout U.S. concert, and at other times, being mesmerized by other artists playing at that famous gathering place, such as Joe Cocker, Van Morrison, and Buffy Sainte-Marie. It was spectacular.

However, our fun-loving hippie hearts yearned to do more in a world that was changing so rapidly, even we couldn't keep up. Since we were voices of peace and love, we wanted to deepen our experience with nature. We decided to accept an offer for Jay to work on an Australian sheep ranch, where I could also teach school in the nearby town. The country life appealed to us as we both enjoyed gardening, out-of-doors activities, and writing poetry. Dwelling in love was an amazing lifestyle. We knew our Australian experience would be a family adventure and positively life-changing.

We decided to travel to Australia along Mexico's picturesque scenic tropical coastline. Plus, we had a buyer for our cherished British MGB, cherry red, convertible sportscar in Mexico City, where the resale was considerably higher than in the States. By Labor Day weekend, we had sold everything we owned and took to the open road. We were answering the call of a greater commission than either of us understood. In our hearts, we knew that together, in love, we were always better.

Our first stop was Mazatlán, Mexico, where we rented a darling bungalow on the beach, ate at the Shrimp Bucket, and met other American travelers. We were introduced to a nearby island where young people from all over the world were staying. Although in the United States, the summer days were slowly merging into autumn, the tropical weather was still hypnotically warm, intriguing, and idyllically romantic.

One of these endless summer nights found us staying over with friends on the island. Waking on the ocean, I watched Jay net fish with the local fishermen whom we shared our morning coffee and sweet pan bread. Upon our return by ferry, we were shocked to discover our sweet MGB was missing. To no avail, we looked everywhere, filed a police report, and even put up posters with a reward for its return.

This inspired us to cling even more to one another, believe everything would work out for the best as, after all, our love for one another was still absolutely magic. With the oceanside bungalow's rent coming to a close, we refused to give up on our dreams. In a meditative stroll dedicated to guidance, every evening, we walked the beach. During one of our sunset walks, we were approached by two visiting yachtsmen who had run into trouble on the eighth annual Invitational L.A. to Mazatlán boat race. Their motor had completed failed them when they had to be towed into the harbor. To procure another motor, required a return trip to the States yet, due to other commitments, and the costs involved, they could not get back to Mazatlán until after Christmas. They asked us to live on their yacht, assured us their larders were full, and we would be paid for doing so.

Love answered our prayers as this would give us time to find the culprits who stole our sweet ride, continue writing, and exploring nature. We were surprised their boat was parked next to the Mexican Navy's only sea-going ship with such a friendly crew on board. It was also within a stone's throw of Pacifico Beer's main brewery, which served oysters on the half-shell and a pint for a peso daily.

While dry-docked, we decorated the living quarters with the luxurious fabrics given to me by a Parisian fashion interior designer who was by then, on her way to South America. The elegant French textiles were satin, silks, and velvets, whose luxurious patterns consisted of exquisite emerald green, brilliant cobalt blues, and rich wine hues.

She also left glass lanterns, strings of beads, and gorgeous over-stuffed pillows. Once it was completed, it reminded us of a romantic gypsy coach. Little did we know, it was a precious prelude of our future eleven years invested in the adventures of RV-ing. Oh, yes, love was forever finding a wonder-filled way.

For our elegant Thanksgiving dinner, we enjoyed a smoked turkey. We broke garlic bread with Canadians and fellow Americans celebrating the opportunity to travel and experience life in other cultures. Right before Christmas, the yachtsmen returned earlier than expected. That exact day, we were asked to move into a charming seaside cottage. The renters were called back because of a family illness in Florida. They had prepaid through the following summer, and although they could not get a refund, they were allowed to gift it forward. The synchronicity was profound!

We arrived to discover a fifty-pound bag of brown rice, a pantry full of essentials, and of course, daily Mercado visits yielded homemade tortillas, fruits to juice and to eat, and excellent farm to market vegetables. Every morning found us having a coffee at the Copa de Leche, walking the coast where Jay would throw out a line and bring in a Bonita fish for dinner. Remember the *I Ching* scholar from L.A.? He was giving classes in the town's historic square. Yes, the power of love is magical.

For the next forty-two years, until my beloved Jay's transition, we lived our lives in this manner. We were blessed with four children, and now, fourteen grandchildren, ages twenty-eight to six years young. I am in awe of our living legacy, humbled that these precious ones call me either Baby Poppa, NiNi, and/or Gawni. I am deeply grateful to walk in beauty, grace, and gratitude, and that our dream continues to unfold per the magical power of love.

Sharyn Jordan is a Feng Shui expert, published author, and entrepreneur. Her current project is designing inspiring environments for writers. Having created, grown, and sold the four start-up companies of Rosebud Preschool, Inc., Maid for You, LLC, Lakeside Entertainment Group, Inc. (movie theatres in the White Mountains) and Seven Streams of Energy, LLC, Sharyn understand the value of doing business from the heart. In 1994, she certified as a Feng Shui practitioner and continues to be internationally known as The Home Whisperer. Her Legacy Series includes the books: *My Sister St. Suzanne, Book of Nathaniel, Dreaming True, My Last Will & Testament*, and *Feng Shui Simplified: Treasures of the Inner & Outer Home*. Email: Classroom@FengShuiSimplied.com. Phone: 480.818.2833.

The Love I Was Missing
By Priya Kalra

"Love is a feeling you can't explain, It tickles your heart and messes with your brain". Unknown

That is a poem I once read when I was young. Oh my, was I dumb.

Because love to me now is more than just a feeling, It's a strong vibration that has brought me deep healing. Let me take you on my journey to find love,
It's not like the movies where you see a white dove.

The meaning of love changed throughout my life. The tickles turning into prickles at times. Unexplainable feelings that cut like a knife. Is this what I fought to strife?

There has to be more to love, I thought. For this is not what I sought.

Where's that love they all talk about?
It had to be somewhere without a doubt.

I searched for it everywhere I went, but always came back to repent.
Why was love running away from me? This is not where I longed to be.

Is there something wrong with me? I needed the answer to set me free. Where do I go from here?
I have nothing to lose but fear!

I needed to water my tree of love, which was drying from up above.

Love Meets Life

There had to be some light,
'Coz I wasn't going down without a fight!

Answers were not that easy to find,
But I needed to get my peace of mind.
So I set out on a soulful journey, searching for something
sweet like honey.

Everything happens in life for a reason. I believe in that
without any treason. My new mantra of meditation,
Gave me hope and inspiration.

Then cancer took over my life, leaving me with the will to
thrive. I was forced to go deep within, The only choice was
to win.

Feeling racked with despair,
I quietly said a daily prayer. Asking God to please help me,
Where's the love I longed to see?

Then it all dawned on me,
Love is not a thing, you see.
It has to be felt, don't you agree? I think I may have found
the key!

For I was seeking love outside, but all this time it was
inside. Buried deep inside my heart, waiting for me to see
the art.

I had to change that ordinary life that I once saw with my
teary eye. Someone's waiting to embrace me, love me for
who I'm meant to be.

The mystery of the dark night was ready to fall out of sight.
I was being drawn closer,
To find the mysterious poser.

Who could be waiting on the other side? Oh my! Oh my!
how much I cried!
I was excited to see who it might be
To my surprise, I couldn't believe it was *me*!

Priya was born in India, raised in Zambia-Africa, and has lived in Arizona-USA for 15 years now. She is a wife, mother, and entrepreneur and lives by the mantra, "Everything happens for a reason!"

Having lived, shared, and embraced different cultures in my life, I have learned the only thing that is really needed is love, but most importantly, self-love! I am now on a simple mission to spread love by teaching meditation and speaking about my cancer journey that's made me fall in love with myself and who I am today!

That Fateful Day In May: A Love Story
By Cindy Kaufman

It was May 1st, 2000, a day I would come to know as "that fateful day in May." That day began innocently enough. I had no idea when I woke up that morning that my life would change forever. That afternoon, my 8-year-old daughter and I went on a bike ride, stopping at the lake to look around before heading back home. After parking our bikes, I sat down on a rocky outcrop near the edge of the lake while my daughter explored nearby.

Looking out upon the lake, I was appreciating the peacefulness when I heard a man's voice say, "Seen any alligators today?" Startled, I looked up, and standing next to me was a man I did not know. I quickly surveyed him to see that he was wearing dress pants, a dress shirt, and a tie. His hands were on his hips, and he was smiling down at me. "No," I replied, "I haven't seen any today." I turned my gaze back out to the lake, assuming he would walk away, but he didn't.

The man began making small talk with me, asking if I came to the lake often and what I thought about the chapel, or meditation building, that would soon be built on the site. I stood up to talk to him as I could see he was not going away. We both agreed that we didn't like the thought of putting a building in such a natural area.

He then asked me if I worked on campus. Most people I met assumed I worked there. After all, I was a woman in my 30s and didn't look like a university student. I explained that I was a student, just finishing my undergraduate degree in psychology and beginning my graduate work in counseling in the fall. I asked what he did, and he shared that he was a Professor of Engineering. We introduced ourselves and continued chatting.

At some point, the man brought up the fact that he was involved with a group that was helping to make people's lives easier and fulfilling their dreams. He talked about the company, which I had never heard of, and said that if I was interested in getting more information, we could set up a time to meet. I had no idea what he was talking about. Still, being a full-time student, a full-time mother of two, and working a part-time job, I had no interest or time for anything else. And besides, I was making my dreams come true by returning to school to pursue my education!

We had been conversing for about 10 minutes or so when I got this strange feeling. Something was happening. I wasn't sure exactly what it was, but I felt this odd sense of knowing, this awareness that this man had just walked into my life for a reason, but what was it? I had been single for about two years, dating off and on, but this man was wearing a wedding ring. Okay, I thought, so it's not that! Whatever it was, I couldn't shake the feeling.

My daughter approached and asked if we could continue our bike ride. I introduced my daughter to the man and explained that I needed to go. We said our goodbyes, but as I got on my bike to ride away, I was still struck by this feeling that there was more to our meeting. I thought to myself, *please, let him stop me from leaving.* I was afraid I would never see him again, and I was certain this was not supposed to be the end. He did not stop me.

That evening, I got online to see if he was who he said he was. Sure enough, he was listed as a Professor of Engineering in the university directory. I couldn't stop that gnawing feeling that we had met for a reason. I found his email address, and I drafted an email that said, "If you are the person I met at the lake this afternoon, I thought our conversation ended too soon. But I won't say more until I hear back from you."

I could not sleep that night. Early the next morning, I checked my email, and he had replied, "Yes, we met at the lake yesterday afternoon, and I, too, thought our conversation ended too soon." He then explained that he wanted to talk to me some more about the company. After a couple more email exchanges, I realized he had been prospecting me for a multilevel marketing venture. I was embarrassed. I had misinterpreted whatever strange thing I had felt. I explained that I was not interested in multilevel marketing, and I didn't care to meet with him. I assumed that would be the end of our emails. It was not the end of our emails.

Over time, I realized that I had not misinterpreted what I felt. Turns out, I had met the love of my life, and he, his! My intuition was spot on that day, but perhaps in poor timing. It took a while, and a whole lot had to happen for us to find this truth that he *was* supposed to walk into my life that day.

Fast forward three and a half years to November 15, 2003, past a lot more story that will not fit here. Remember I said we had chatted about a chapel or meditation center being built at the lake? We got married in that building!

Fast forward 15 more years to November 15, 2018, past a whole lot more story, and we returned to that building to renew our vows on our 15th wedding anniversary. That building is called The Baughman Center, and it sits on Lake Alice on the University of Florida campus in Gainesville, Florida. On that fateful day in May, four words changed my life forever: Seen any alligators today?

Cindy Kaufman, MEd, EdS, brings her background in counselor education and 25 years as a hospice volunteer to her work as a certified end of life doula, death educator, and international best-selling author. Cindy is the owner of HeartSpeak End of Life Companioning LLC, and President of The Colorado End-of-Life Collaborative. She serves as a compassionate companion on life's final journey for the dying person and their loved ones. Her book, *The Mortal's Guide to Dying Well—Practical Wisdom from an End of Life Doula*, is available on Amazon.com. Based in Denver, Colorado, contact Cindy at www.heartspeak2u.com.

Playing For Love
By Dana Keller

"I am a tree!" I stated boldly to the group of adults as I threw my arms (branches) into the air. Another person joined me in our "stage" area: "I am a person sitting under the tree," he said, and plopped down next to my feet, leaning against my legs (trunk). "I am a squirrel," said another person, joining the two of us, hands to mouth as if busily chewing on a nut. "I'll take the person," I stated, exiting the scene with the "person," leaving the squirrel to stand alone.

It was 1999. The "person" and I were married (and still are), and at the time had two young sons. The scene I just described was an activity in a beginning improv class for adults. While I had an extensive history with performing, my husband—an accountant—did not. Together, we were learning how to be creative in the moment and how to say "yes, and..." to whatever arose.

Earlier that year, Jim had gone on a business trip to Vietnam. He was working for a company that was opening health care clinics in Southeast Asia, so he'd been traveling in the area a few times—in fact, on one trip, the boys and I were able to join him in Kuala Lumpur, Malaysia. It was an incredible experience, and he enjoyed the work, despite the long trips away from our family. However, after this last trip to Vietnam, something was different.

He immediately became quite ill. He stayed in bed for a week, shades drawn. He mostly slept, and very occasionally, I could get him to have some broth or some small meal. After weeks of not seeing any improvement, he decided to see our family doctor. Many months of testing later, Dr. Stevens sat us down.

"Jim," he began, "We've ruled out virtually everything physical that could be causing your distress. In my professional opinion, I think that what you are dealing with," he paused, "is clinical depression." What? This was a possibility we hadn't considered. I mean, he wasn't "sad"—his stomach didn't feel right. Sure, there was sleeplessness and lack of appetite, but surely that was due to some physical issue, not *depression.*

Just before his trip to Vietnam, I had been seeing a therapist myself for anxiety and general malaise. In one session, she asked me what I love to do, and I replied, "Sing!" to which she replied, "Go sing!" Although I had very little vocal experience and had a hard time carrying a tune, I followed her advice, joining a community vocal group, and taking voice lessons.

As I sang each week, I found that I felt lighter, happier. Rehearsal was a time of connecting with others, laughing, and joining our voices in (sometimes not so perfect) harmonies. It made my brain focus on the fun task at hand and the voices in the group rather than the ones in my head. It's hard to sing and still be sad!

When Jim's depression diagnosis finally sunk in, he began seeing my therapist. While some serious emotional work and medication were helping him make progress, he was still really struggling. The therapist told him, "You need to laugh." He probably shouldn't have told me, because that's what compelled me to sign us up for the improv class being offered by our oldest son's drama teacher.

I'd done theater at school and in the community, but never improv. It scared the crap out of me! As I said before, Jim didn't have any performance background, but I think he felt too miserable to care. He was having a hard time functioning so I could have signed him up for dancing with llamas, and he would have gone along with me.

Over the next few weeks, we learned about improv together. We had *fun*. We connected with other people, it got us out of the house, and we learned some important improv rules (yes, improv has rules) that it turns out are not only great for improv, but for life as well. Jim found in improv what I found while singing—when he was busy laughing, playing, learning, connecting, his brain had much less time to worry. It kept his focus off his own struggle for a short little window of time, and sometimes that little window can make all the difference.

These experiences are what taught me the importance of play throughout our lives. Play isn't just about having fun, it's about learning and *loving*. It gets us out of our heads and into our hearts and bodies. With everything going on in our society that is contentious, play can help us connect and bridge the gaps—and have fun while doing it!

Play can take many shapes and forms—it doesn't have to be arts-based, but the arts (especially for us "non-artists") are a great way to tap into play. As part of completing my master's degree a few years ago, I defined play as "the joy of being fully present and engaged in the process, without fear of failure—a pleasant venture into the unknown." In my research, I found that (for adults) play could be sports, needlepoint, fishing, hiking, computer games—any number of activities. However, many adults found those activities to be most playful if they were done with a group of people, if they were being spontaneous or learning something new, and if they weren't attached to a specific outcome.

Jim and I only took that one six-week improv class, but it was an important part of the foundation of our marriage. It's hard to believe we've been married 30 years this year, and that class was over 20 years ago! With time, work, and medication, he's managed to mostly stave off any more bouts of depression. Taking the time to play helped us both individually and as a couple. "I am a tree!" and I still choose this "person" as my play-mate for life

Dana Keller, MA, is a writer, speaker, and advocate for play across the lifespan. As an InterPlay® leader-in-training, she creates playful experiences where adults can explore connections with their minds, bodies, emotions, and other participants. Her passion is changing the world through play and education. You can reach Dana at www.danakeller.net.

Love Is Black Liberation
By Chris Love

When asked to contribute to a book about love, I thought it would be easy. I mean, my last name *is* Love. But now, as I sit down to put words to the page, I find myself and my People in the midst 2 crises which threaten our ability to simply exist—the Coronavirus and racism. This is a time of great suffering that will be retold as history to my grandchildren, my great-grandchildren, and my great-great-grandchildren, until one day it is forgotten and then repeated. That Black people "can't breathe" has a double meaning that I wish my progeny will never have to know from experience, as I am certain my ancestors wished for me.

Yet, through the heaviness I've felt cooped up during a pandemic, while simultaneously watching as a revolution is born, it isn't hard to sense that love is at the core of everything happening around me.

Love is taking care of the community. Whether providing mutual aid or organizing bail funds, we are moved to take care of our communities at a time where our governments have intentionally failed us. We cook and deliver food. We send funds through payment apps. We sew masks. We chant together. We comfort each other. We wipe away the tears and teargas. We stand united, calling for the recognition of our humanity while ensuring that the basic needs of our communities are met.

Love is intimacy. It's the closeness of quarantining with your husband and 3 kids indefinitely and not killing them as you realize you wouldn't want to be stuck with anyone else. It's sharing the same space for homeschooling and conference calls, coffee and homemade cookies (as you have time to bake). It is when your husband sneaks off to post on his Twitter that he loves you simply because you exist. It's playing dancing games with your youngest and talking Black liberation with your teenagers. It's video calls with your sister who lives across the country, joking about her newest caftan because "nobody has time for pants in a pandemic."

Love is self-care. It's ugly crying with relief when your doctor tells you that you don't have Coronavirus. It's feeling acknowledged when the same doctor says you are experiencing anxiety. It is unplugging from social media and finding joy in doing absolutely nothing. It's listening to your favorite song on repeat for hours and singing at the top of your lungs. It's laughing when your little one tickles your toes. It's "calling in Black" on Juneteenth. It's cutting yourself some slack when you're failing and flailing at being a supermom during a pandemic.

Love is accountability. It's when we use #SayHerName as a cry for a more inclusive movement for Black lives—one that lifts up black trans and cis women, and gender non-conforming folx. Love is when we call on our Black fathers, brothers, and sons to do better by Black womxn in general. Love is when we ask our parents and grandparents to push through respectability and explain to them that it is rooted in white supremacy. It's compassionately challenging your lifelong friends when they repost an offensive meme on social media and hitting "unfriend" when they lash out at you defensively.

My heart is engorged with love, but I still yearn for a love that looks like Black liberation. Black liberation must feel like being unbound by a disease that attacks Black bodies at alarming rates, not because our bodies are inherently, but because of racism that creates inequities in our healthcare system. It must feel like walking down the street without fear of dying because of racism that creates inequities in policing. It must feel like reversing the damage done over 400 years of subjugation and second-class citizenship. It must feel like freedom from a colonized mindset that has taught me that I must be inferior, even though I don't quite understand why.

Black liberation is true love. It is the only love that I have not experienced in my lifetime, yet I will spend the rest of my lifetime marching toward it.

Chris Love is a tribal attorney and unapologetic reproductive justice advocate. Chris has dedicated her legal career to serving tribal governments and enterprises in Arizona and throughout the Southwest. Additionally, Chris proudly serves as the Board Chair for Planned Parenthood Advocates of Arizona, the political advocacy and education organization that supports the work of Planned Parenthood health clinics in her state. Chris lives in Chandler, Arizona, with her husband and three children, who are all community activists in their own right.

Steps Toward A Revolution Of The Heart
By Nora Malfettone

Self-love is the most selfless state to be in. Shame is the most selfish state. I know that this might seem backward or ironic to some, but allow me to unpack this notion.

Self-love is detachment from self-judgment. It's giving oneself the freedom to feel worthy and therefore receive love and emotional nourishment in a way that is needed to thrive. Self-love is detachment from identifying oneself with one's own story, or experience, and the idea that one's own past defines them.

Coming into self-love means to recognize that one can grow and learn without punishment from one's self. When one is in a state of self-love, they are open to listening, to seeing objectively, and to being more compassionate. Self-love gives one permission to work through emotions and to self-regulate without criticism. Self-love is the ability to make appropriate decisions for one's well-being to show up in the healthiest way for the betterment of their family, friends, community, and world.

Shame is created by the sense of being unworthy of love because of self-criticism. It's debilitating, not only for personal growth, but the growth of relationships and collective. It revolves around the idea that true love *has* conditions. Love is the most natural energy and is not associated with the judgment of the mind. Shame creates defensiveness and divisiveness.

It closes off the ability for one to see, hear, or feel naturally, with wisdom. Instead, they exist and interpret through a filter of their own wound. When one feels ashamed and unworthy of love, I imagine their life force, their well-being, feels threatened. They would be more triggered into violence and aggression towards themselves and others. Shame limits the spirit into its expansion toward its full potential by shackling the mind (and therefore one's awareness) to the confines of one's own story. I believe if everyone healed themselves of collective shame, we'd experience ourselves, and each other, with much more beauty and allow love in without resistance.

The disruptive energy that forbids the receptivity of self-love is shame.

Working through and dismantling the burden of shame is something that I've been doing for myself my entire life and have been helping others do the same for over fifteen years as a transformational healer, energy worker, and doula. Something I've learned in my experience is that one must be willing to have the courage and curiosity to explore who they are without attachment to the shame they carry with them.

Curiosity and inquiry open up perceptions of excitement and adventure in pursuit of simply a new experience. It awakens a childlike viewpoint, as it's not challenging or pressuring the mind to believe anything specifically. Curiosity evokes an awareness and presence like a newborn baby.

I implore myself, those I work with, and *you* to explore with curiosity the sensations in and around your body.

Have the courage to explore deeper into parts of yourself that you have numbed, avoided, haven't fully acknowledged, or noticed. Breathe. Breath is key in allowing oneself to dive deeper into one's own conscious-ness.

I've learned it to be called *"witness consciousness,"* the ability to be aware of one's inner and/or outer environment without judgment. Awareness, to me, is fundamental in the ability to be present and to release the mental attachment to shame. Awareness is using the five senses: sound, sight, touch, taste, and smell to act as tools to fully connect to the present moment, without the mind's chatter. Using inner awareness to acknowledge all parts of one's self without judgment, opens up the possibility for one to organically love themselves.

"Love is the absence of judgment." ~ the Dalai Lama XIV

When one has full awareness of their inner and outer environments, they can then feel grounded in the ability to be authentic, live, and speak their truth. With full awareness of the inner and outer environment, a blend of the two occurs. One's identity does not then feel threatened, as this identity was based on a dual view or one which no longer exists with an awareness of both at once. The outer environment then becomes synonymous or in-tandem with the inner.

One expands their sense of identity in a way that no longer *needs* to be protected, as they now understand it to not be isolated and instead wholly flexible. This lack of dependency, and therefore lack of desire to hold solid allows this very room to feel, live, and empathize with the experiences of others. When people feel free and safe to be in their authentic expression, there's then natural room for compassion, empathy, and understanding.

Without harboring shame, one would be able to have healthy relationships by witnessing others with compassion for who they are. There would be no impetus to take things personally because they would have deep roots in knowing who they are fundamentally.

When people heal themselves of shame, there will be more conscious leadership in communities. Our communities will be led by those who speak with honesty and integrity because of the conscious awareness that they've cultivated of their inner and outer environment. When one feels liberated in these capacities, a person can then thrive, not just survive or tolerate life.

These leaders and individuals would genuinely be able to celebrate their own existence and the existence of all of life. Being liberated of shame would mean being liberated of self-judgment, and inevitably mean non-judgment of others. In this way, our creative capacities are unleashed, and we remember our innocence, purity, and beauty.

"Complacency is the death of the soul."
~ Janaya 'Future' Khan.

For one to truly make a difference in this world, for one to truly be selfless, they must be willing to disappoint all those who believe that love has conditions. One must be willing to put down the burden of others' projected shame and realize that it was never their responsibility to carry. We can then move through the fear of witnessing our *own* magnificence—which is not confined—and surrender into the unknown expansion into love.

Nora Malfettone is a certified yoga teacher, Jikiden Reiki Master and Teacher, birth doula, Ayurvedic wellness counselor, aesthetician, personal trainer, and mother. She's a trained classical singer, sound healer, clairvoyant and clairsentient. She has been devoted to her dharma as a healer and spiritual teacher for over 15 years. Her multi-disciplined methodology and personal experience offer a unique, holistic, compassionate, custom approach to facilitating deep transformation and healing for those who work with her.

Contact: NoraMalfettone.com, noramalfettone@gmail.com, or 203-913-0497.

The Beautiful Dance
By Cindy Mallory

Only from the heart can you touch the sky. —Rumi

I look at my mother's face, hoping for a glimmer of recognition. She's staring at the TV, the dark pupils of her eyes tiny and lifeless. Without dentures, her mouth is turned down at the corners like an upside-down smile. The nursing home took them away for her safety, and now that her diet is mostly liquids, they aren't needed.

I rub the soft skin of her arm.

"Hi, Mom, I'm here."

She pulls her eyes away from the TV and focuses on me, her face expressionless. I take a deep breath. "This is going to be hard," I think to myself, fighting back the tears. I live 3,400 kilometers away, and her illness has progressed since I last saw her.

I am thankful for earlier visits when I could take her for walks through the garden, and she was able to say short phrases. Back then, she would gaze at me, and I could feel her presence. Love shone through her eyes. I had been thrilled once when I told her I'd be back in six weeks, and she'd said a whole sentence, "I don't have a calendar."

It had been four years since Mom's diagnosis. By then, at 66 years of age, she was already in full decline. Her early-onset dementia, Pick's disease, had stolen her vibrant personality and her ability to function in her world. She became a stranger who had tantrums and was banned from the local supermarket. The last time I visited before she

120

was moved into the nursing home, her husband showed me a birthday card she'd tried to write. It had taken her four hours, he said, to write the two sentences. The printing was legible, but there was whiteout in several places and missing words, so it didn't quite make sense.

Since then, I've visited as often as I can, savoring every connection, trying to grab hold of the mother who was being erased so quickly.

I look at her again, still hoping for some sign that she knows who I am. As the memories keep coming, one particular visit shines bright. Two years earlier, I'd found her sitting in a large half-circle of residents. In front was a man singing, strumming his guitar to his song. The staff began to get some of the residents up to dance, and one of the support workers came over to Mom.

"Would you like to dance, Marie?" she asked, and Mom nodded eagerly.

"Why don't you dance with your daughter?"

I helped her stand, and we began to waltz slowly together, feet shuffling softly. She gripped my hands, gazing up at me with a peaceful look on her face.

Tears ran down my face as we danced, an awareness that the journey with my mother was winding down. Throughout my adult years, time spent with her had been especially precious, for embedded in each moment was a pain we both felt, a loss that couldn't be fixed. I had lost her when I was five years old. Circumstances beyond our control had pulled us apart during a difficult divorce. One day she had driven away, never to come back. It wasn't until adulthood that I'd gathered the courage to find her. It took two years of searching, and when I finally had her phone number, I gingerly held onto the precious piece of paper like it was the magic door to my mother. It was a door I was afraid to go through. I was sure she wouldn't remember me, or worse, that she hated me. After a sudden family tragedy, in the depths of despair one day, I took the plunge and fished the wrinkled paper out of my pocket. I dialed the number, my heart thudding as a woman answered the phone.

"Hi, you probably don't remember me. My name is Cindy." There was a gasp on the other end of the line.

"*Daughter* Cindy?" she replied, the tremor in her voice catching me by surprise. I heard a chair scrape across the floor in the background. I was shocked that I didn't know her voice.

Yet, from those first moments, there was a bond, from her heart to mine. It felt as if the world was right side up again. When she flew from British Columbia to visit soon after, my brother and I waited anxiously at the bottom of the arrivals escalator at Toronto airport, searching every face, wondering if we would recognize her.

Finally, there she was descending toward us, a short beaming lady with a beautiful, kind face. She was an angel to me, a fairy princess who'd existed in another lifetime. I had a mother. It was beyond belief.

We continued our dance slowly around the clearing in front of the chairs. She smiled at me then, like this was the most perfect moment of her life, and there was nothing more she needed. As we looked into each other's eyes, suddenly, time fell away, and a feeling of pure love took over my whole being. At that moment, the years we'd been apart melted away, and there was only joy. There was only a little girl and her mother dancing.

I jolt back to the present and notice she is staring at me. Are those tears in her eyes? I stroke her arm, hoping they aren't. I don't want her to suffer any more than she already has. Such a double-edged sword, wishing for her to be aware, yet hoping she isn't.

I think about that day we danced, realizing my whole life has been one long dance with my mother, even during her absence. I suddenly feel the beauty in all of it, like a softness that dulls the sharp edges, leaving only the love that has been there all along.

"Goodbye, Mom," I say, tenderly kissing her forehead. In my mind, I see her face smiling at me, and I have everything I need.

Cindy Mallory is a yoga teacher, reiki master, and writer. She is blessed with an amazing husband to share her life. She is on a lifelong healing journey and is inspired by the words of Maya Angelou, "There is no greater agony than bearing an untold story inside of you." She hopes that through finding her voice and living her truth, she can help light the way for others to find their path to healing. Cindy recently contributed a chapter to the book, *The Grateful Soul*, and looks forward to finishing her first book. You can reach her at cindy.mallory@utoronto.ca.

Self-Love For One, Please
By Alicia McBride

I knew I was different from the age of five. I remember being in daycare, sitting cross-legged with my arms out behind me and hands on the floor. A little boy got up, ran around the outside of the circle, and accidentally stepped on my finger. I remember it hurting a little bit. I held my hand and frowned. The teacher looked at me, scrunched up her face with pouty lips, and said, "Did he hurt your little pinky finger?" in baby talk.

I distinctly remember thinking (with attitude), *"Why are you talking to me like that?"* She spoke to me as you would speak to a small child with a "boo-boo." It was perfectly normal. I didn't feel perfectly normal, I felt like an old woman in a five-year-old girl's body. Why wouldn't she talk to me like an adult? Because I wasn't an adult. I just thought I was.

It was a strange imbalance. I felt out of sorts. I felt old. I didn't understand why I was so young, yet it felt like I had lived a thousand years. Even now, I still feel old. That has never gone away, but now I know where it comes from and how to handle it.

Also, when I was little, I blindly believed everything everyone said. When another kid told me I was ugly, I believed them. That was my truth. I was ugly. When someone called me stupid, I believed them. I was stupid. Adults told me to "toughen up," and said I was too sensitive. Okay. I was going to move forward in my life, knowing that I was ugly, stupid, and too sensitive. Got it.

As a teenager, I had a friend tell me that I wasn't her "fun friend." I was the friend that she could talk to and share her feelings with, but I was not fun to be around. I believed her. I believed that I was boring.

There I was, growing up feeling old, ugly, stupid, thin-skinned, and mundane. I'm laughing at this now, but boy was it awful back then. I *hated* myself. I hated the way I looked. I hated the way I felt. I hated how I felt everything. I was too sensitive. I don't remember anyone telling me it was okay to be sensitive. Maybe it happened, but I don't remember. I remember "Toughen up," and "You're okay." I was not okay, thank you. I needed someone to give me permission to be me.

In high school, I found a few friends who showed me unconditional love. They gave me space to be me. Unfortunately, the damage was done, and through a series of events, I spiraled downward anyway.

What happened? I was dejected. I was a wreck. I was suicidal. I tried my best to function, but it didn't work. I didn't understand why I had those feelings. It was a terrible time in my life, but it was a good opportunity for learning and growth. Experiencing the depths of despair gave me a chance to heal my wounds. What did I do? I looked around and realized I didn't want to stay there. Life is a choice.

I chose life, and I picked myself up. *Slowly.* It was brutally slow. But I did it. I kept learning and growing. I practiced self-care. I gave myself space to be me. I allowed myself to feel all of my feelings without judgment. I read an innumerable amount of self-help articles and books. I tried alternative healing methods. I tried acupuncture, reiki, massage, and yoga. I became a certified yoga instructor and a reiki master. I took classes in painting, pottery, and dance. I participated in whatever spoke to me.

I finally listened to my inner voice. You know when you're talking to a friend, and you need to vent? You don't want their opinion, and you don't want them to fix the situation. You just want to get it all out. That's called holding space for someone. When you don't interfere, you encourage them to lay it out and give them the space to do it. I did that for myself. I wrote. I sang. I danced. I gave myself space to figure out who I am. I allowed myself to fall in love with me.

I learned to love myself unconditionally. I learned to love all sides, even the shadows. With unconditional love comes acceptance. Acceptance of who you are now and who you will become. I learned to love and accept who I am. It was hard, and it took longer than I would have liked, but it was worth it.

If this resonates with you, I encourage you to follow your dreams, listen to your inner voice, and to fall in love with yourself. Whoever that is. Be the best you that you can be. Dig deep, find out who you are, and be that person. Love that person. Hold space for yourself and be kind. Say nice things to your body and to your soul.

I encourage you to practice self-care. Make a list of everything you love doing, and when you are feeling down or low, pick something off of that list and do it. Self-care can be as simple as closing your eyes and taking a deep breath, walking outside, or saying "no" to your to-do list. It can be bigger, like taking a vacation or hiking a mountain.

You can take a new class or try something you have always wanted to do but never had the time. Make the time. Making time to heal your soul is worth it. You will feel better. When you are uplifted, those around you feel uplifted too.

I hope my story has helped you in some way. I hope you learn to love yourself. Love all your outstanding qualities, your beauty inside and out, and even your shadows. I hope you accept and love your true self. I love you!

Alicia McBride is a creative clairvoyant empath who loves empowering people to heal themselves, writing books, and being a mom to two energetic boys. She lives in southeastern PA, enjoys dancing, digital painting, and wearing PJ's in public. Alicia also has degrees in Psychology and Interior Design, is a Certified Yoga Instructor, a Reiki Master, and has gone through a Spiritual Awakening (does that ever end?). Her eclectic background continues to inspire her to help others through creative outlets such as writing books and energy healing. Find her online at HealingLightEmpath.com.

Fluid Love In The Sea Of Sadness
By Mairi Moibeal

I was raised in an area that didn't quite understand me. As a child, I felt so deeply in a way I couldn't communicate. Navigating through a small West Virginia town, as an undiagnosed autistic kid, was difficult. Nicknamed "Smiley" in daycare, I was happy and free. I felt love deeply, in waves that would swallow me. I was surrounded by love, but as I grew, the waves revealed pain deeper than I thought I could stand. At the depths of this sea of sadness held the shame of a child living in an area that didn't understand her, and didn't support her.

It became lonely and confusing. Recognizing that I didn't quite fit, I watched others for clues on who to be. I learned what received good reactions, and I learned what got me in trouble. I learned how to be an actress, and I did it well. What I didn't realize was that I was completely leaving myself behind.

By high school, I was sipping on a cocktail of undiagnosed neuro-divergencies, mental illnesses, and addictions. I was also struggling with my sexuality, and I knew from my summers at church camp that my thoughts and feelings were sinful. Being raped taught me that I was disposable and weak. Hiding behind alcohol and sports, I continued to struggle silently, not discussing the pain I was enduring. I tumbled through life, riding big waves of joy, to then being thrown into the darkest of waters.

When I was able to get out of my hometown, I met people that did understand me. I was seen, and I was heard. I learned that the lack of queer representation in my area was not due to the lack of LGBTQ+ folx. The lack of represent-tation was from the fear and lack of safety in that area to live our truths and tell our stories.

In those next years, as I fumbled through college and continued to struggle to fit into society, I knew that there had to be a better way to live. I continued checking off boxes that society deems successful, but the waves in the sea of sadness got choppy and harsh. For a moment, I got lost at sea, capsized, and was unable to come up for air.

During my darkest nights, in my internal sea, I sat alone. In that solitude, I found healing and love. When I was alone, I was free. When I was alone, I was able to connect to my truth. It wasn't until I realized that I was allowed to be myself that I was able to breathe underwater in the depths of the sea. It was during that time that I connected to my favorite type of love. Like water, this love was fluid and calming, but it was powerful. This love caressed me on the surface and held me tight through the strong tides. I allowed it to lift me and pull me under. In the depths of the waters, I found my shame spaces. Like buried treasure, I would bring them to the surface. I would examine and hold them gently, allowing time with each piece. My shame spaces, my shadows, provide me guidance on what needs to be nurtured in my life. This fluid love helps me navigate my sea of sadness. By meeting my shadows, I learned to understand and cherish them, while incorporating them to honor my duality.

Fluid love is the ability to ride the waves of life and feel strong in your purpose. It is finding a moment to pause and acknowledge each wave for what it brings to you. It is trust and love for yourself. It is accepting and honoring, as opposed to judging. We each have an innate sense to heal, and we can do so if we pause to listen to ourselves.

I allowed others to put me in uncomfortable boxes. Until I found love in every wave of life, I kept getting knocked down in my sea of sadness. Love exists in all emotions and every wave. As I integrate new parts of myself that I have shunned, I am able to gain wisdom, reclaim my power, and release shame.

My sea of sadness is now my place of self-love and healing. When the outside world is overwhelming, I remind myself that I can breathe in the solitude. Even when the waves are big, and the depth seems infinite, I know there is love flowing inside. Through our lived experiences, we gain the tools to be able to live in our truth and better advocate for our needs. The darkness is a gift that strengthens the light if we choose to assimilate it.

We are here to find and integrate our buried treasures from the depths of our deep seas.

I was programmed to think my feelings were wrong, and that the way my mind worked wasn't okay. I felt alone, misunderstood, and ashamed. I was tired, exhausted from fighting the waves. I hadn't yet realized that by finding peace in chaos, by way of fluid love and shadow integration, I wouldn't have to fight as hard to keep my head above water. I can breathe under there while I take a peek at my buried treasures.

I still feel sadness for my younger self, but she is no longer alone or misunderstood. We have the ability to heal and evolve. Being queer is part of what makes me beautiful, unique, and powerful. Being autistic is part of what makes me determined, empathic, and smart. My resiliency is what brought me the fluid love that comes with riding the waves of life. When I'm connected to myself, my purpose and my truth keep me securely supported at sea. Part of my purpose is to share my story for the people who still don't see enough of themselves in the world. The sea of sadness is where I heal and share my story. You matter, and your story matters, too.

Mairi Moibeal, she/they
@mmhealingservices
mairimoibeal@gmail.com
Mairi Moibeal is a healing guide, shadow worker, and intuition coach. Mairi owns Mairi Moibeal Healing Services, where she and her husband use their education, training, gifts, and experience to guide others through their healing journey.

The Dress That Changed Everything
By Chelsa Morrison She/Her/Hers

"**M**om, can I wear my purple dress on the first day of school?" We are driving, and my kiddo is chatting away like any other five-year-old excited to start kindergarten. My stomach drops immediately, my fear for her palpable. See, for two years, my daughter has kept a secret from most in our community.

"What if someone makes fun of you?" I asked. She sits quietly, thinking about this. I know she's thinking of neighbors and preschool classmates who don't know who she is. My kiddo wanted to wear her favorite dress that she loved to wear, no matter the weather. Keep in mind, this dress was wool, and we lived in Texas at the time. Of course, she would pick that dress. But, you have to understand, the dress didn't scare me, other's reactions did.

Our daughter was born transgender. She knew it, we knew it, and our circle of friends knew it as well. But the world didn't know—yet.

Our daughter decided that fateful day (at age 5, mind you) to pretend to be a boy for another two years at school until she couldn't pretend any longer. The anxiety between living authentically at home, but not being able to at school was making her ill, both physically and emotionally. One day, in the second grade, she'd had enough. She came home and lost it. All of these feelings that she held in every day exploded at home. She was crying and yelling that she's "tired of pretending to be a boy at school. I always have to worry if I said it right, did I do it like a boy, did I out myself?"

There are many moments on this beautiful journey that stick out, but this is the one that turned me into an activist for trans and non-binary youth.

We pulled our kiddo out of school and found a wonderful practice with incredible therapists who helped us. Our therapist already had a handful of parents that met every other Saturday, while our kids did activities and were spoiled rotten with sugar by another therapist. It was so fun to hear their laughter outside, running through the halls during our group sessions. It was always a reminder that our kids are happy. Those Saturdays were a lifeline for our family and us. Our kids now had friends that were trans, and hopefully, they didn't feel so alone. For many of us, the group became our family. From 2015 to our move in 2017, we spent holidays, birthdays, and monthly socials in our homes. We went to conferences and training together to help us become stronger advocates for our kiddos.

In 2016, a handful of us stood in front of our local media and attempted to educate others on how and why "bathroom" bills are harmful and nothing but fear-mongering. That same year, our daughter was asked to help carry the Equality Texas banner for her first Pride. We were surrounded by friends and our chosen family that day, and it was hotter than hell but perfect! I'll never forget driving into the parade line and our daughter seeing all the rainbows and gender-affirming signs. She exclaimed, "Mom, I totally belong here!"

I'm glad she had a great time because we had no idea how awful things would get in the coming months when our legislature was back in session. My daughter and our friends were being used as political pawns and at the expense of their very safety and well-being. While Sky is the reason we became activists, we stayed for all the friends we met that are now family. We have now lobbied in three states for trans youth. We have spoken out at rallies, panels, conferences, and national groups to share our story so that others will help us in this fight. We show up whenever and however we can because my daughter's community is in jeopardy. Black trans women, especially, are being killed at a sickening rate.

We want a safe world for our daughter and our friends, but we need your help. Please consider joining your state Equality organization. You will get an added education on community efforts, policies, and other ways you can get involved. You have all met someone who is transgender or non-conforming as they have been here since the beginning of time. I have more gratitude than I can express for our daughter's elders in the community. They took us in when our blood families turned their backs and are committed to fighting hard for all of our kids.

Our daughter is now 12, and she is thriving. She's her own best advocate and has now done a few speaker panels while we sit in the audience and cheer her on. She's a kind, confident, and well-spoken little warrior. She wants you to know that if you just get to know her, you'll love her.

We couldn't agree more.

Chelsa Morrison is a mama-bear activist for LGBTQ kiddos. She fights for her daughter and transgender and non-binary youth. Her goal is to let other transgender youth and their families know that they are not alone, and she hopes that by joining together and pressing forward, we can ensure safety for our LGBTQ kids and community. You can reach Chelsa Morrison at chelsamorrison@yahoo.com.

From Bracelet To Banner
By Grace Murdock

"Success is attaining your dream while helping others to benefit from that dream materializing."
—Sugar Ray Leonard

A dream from a nightmare is not a path I ever want to take again. The sustaining outcomes of this dream are people and the relationships that had been forged before its beginning, and the message all will take forward to share with others. My mother's most precious piece of advice her entire life was, "Surround yourself with people who raise you up and *be* one of those people." Thank you, Mom! My story is about people helping kindness win—first, the nightmare.

On December 14, 2012, between 9:35 and 9:40 AM, 26 lives were lost at the hands of a single gunman at Sandy Hook Elementary School in Newtown, Connecticut, where my niece Beth resides with her family. As soon as the news was broadcast, I called Beth, and we cried along with millions of others.

A single Facebook post about Mr. Rogers' mother telling him, "In times of tragedy always look for the helpers," launched me into action. As a former educator, I had the uncanny feeling that the children and staff lost at the school were my responsibility, and I felt called to become a helper. I had to help change the focus from tragedy to hope. I scoured the internet researching a wearable object. I discovered a way to string beads on a bracelet to help the wearer count kind acts. Kindness benefits us in three ways through giving, receiving, and just witnessing it. I ordered supplies, made a dozen bracelets, sent them to Beth in Newtown, and asked her to pass them to anyone she felt could use one. I wish I could have sent a thousand.

I called my creation, "Kindness Bracelet, the original." The bracelet had a special interactive bonus of allowing the wearers to slide 12 beads along the cord toward a kindness charm for every kind act they experienced each day. With every bead moved toward the kindness charm, hope was realized. Before I knew it, I had created a Kindness Bracelet factory in my home. Friends, family, and a single retailer helped launch my business.

Early in this journey, I had to determine what to do with the revenue. I had an epiphany to donate all profits and thus began the next wave of euphoric kindness ripples that touched hearts and honored the lost hearts at Sandy Hook.

Surprise donations were made to people in need, local causes, and bracelets were donated to school and church auctions. I sent bracelets around the world with friends going on mission trips to share with the people they met. The giving of the bracelets put me on a "helper's high," and I wanted others to experience the joy through sharing kindness.

While researching material for Salisbury's inaugural TEDx event where I presented a talk on "Kindness in'Act'ion," I met wonderful people online from all over the U.S. and Canada who were already on their own kindness journeys. They became mentors, and I learned much from them on how to become a Kindness Influencer on social media. Their kindness helped me gain the confidence to pursue every opportunity to spread kindness, and our friendships remain strong these seven years later.

One day I found a story about Buddy Benches on playgrounds where children sit at recess if they don't have a play partner. The entire student body knows that if they see a lonesome student, someone needs to go ask him or her to play. I contacted friends in the school system and received permission to place benches on every playground in Wicomico County. My bracelet funds bought the materials, and the students enrolled in woodworking classes built the benches. It was meaningful for the older students to know they were helping younger children to enjoy recess while learning kindness and compassion.

My bracelet revenue brought several internationally known kindness speakers to our schools from New York, Cape Cod, California, and Florida. One of these personalities was Orly Wahba of Life Vest Inside, who created the worldwide Dance for Kindness. Seeing the impact of the dance on YouTube, I immediately asked Mayor Jacob Day if he could clear a street for Salisbury to participate. His first "yes" in 2016 laid the groundwork for dances 2016-2019 plus every kind community unifying activity after that. In fact, I went to the mayor so often to request permission for kindness activities that he honored me with the title of City of Salisbury's Secretary of Kindness.

In 2017, I found my dream while reading about the World Kindness Movement. I discovered there was a way to have our city named a World Kindness USA City. Ten Kindness Performance Indicators (KPIs) had to be satisfied, and Salisbury had already accomplished 6 of the 10. We had our City Council sign a unanimous resolution to imbed kindness in all city decisions. By 2019, we had accomplished all the KPIs, and the City of Salisbury was named the 1st World Kindness USA City. Dream realized!

There have been valuable benefits to our journey. We are most grateful for Kindness Clubs in our elementary and middle schools. Our mayor commissioned #kindSBY to be Salisbury's official kindness body for the city with 20 Kindness Commissioners who work tirelessly spreading kindness. My non-profit, "Wicomico grows Kindness," continues to work closely with groups around the county, promoting kindness and donating funds. Our city's branding includes kindness for everyone.

To all my helpers, my friends, our generous donors, my family, and my Partners in Kind, thank you with all my heart. We are helping kindness win. We are continuing because community unity through kindness is our dream, and more work needs to be done.

Oh, and the banner…just come and see our 20' X 4' banner naming Salisbury as the 1st World Kindness USA City.

WE ARE #kindSBY, *Where kindness lives.*

Grace has lived on the eastern shore of Maryland her entire life. Grace created a Kindness Bracelet, the original in 2013, which set her on a kindness path. She is the founder of her non-profit, Wicomico grows Kindness.

As the Secretary of Kindness for the City of Salisbury, she brought events and speakers to her community to help everyone adopt kindness as their first option when interacting with others.

www.kindsby.com
Facebook: Grace Foxwell Murdock
Wicomico grows Kindness
Kindness Bracelet
Kind SBY
Instagram:kindsby_kindnessbracelet

Is Love The Answer?
By Laura Murphy

This extraordinary world we live in offers so much beauty, yet it feels like it is riddled with problems: climate change, political divide, violence, gender inequality, racism, food and water scarcity, habitat destruction, and species extinction, to name a few. I have always cared deeply about making a positive impact on the world. But given the complexities of these systemic problems that have been developing for centuries, and with so much power held by political and corporate entities, how could I possibly do anything to make a difference? It can feel overwhelming, and even at times, hopeless. I have flirted with the temptations of apathy—to simply throw my arms up in the air and make the best of my time here. But I know it only becomes hopeless when I decide not to take responsibility to grow and learn how to do my part; how to be part of the solution. But where do I begin?

It occurred to me during a time of reflection that perhaps there is a simple solution. An answer that draws on our innate human wisdom. Something easily accessible, yet so powerful it could create a shift in the world. The answer is love. Love is the way to empowerment. I started to envision a world with more love. A world where love simply does not allow us to tolerate many of today's issues such as environmental degradation and human injustice and suffering.

This calls into question, what is love? And how can it become the most effective solution to our troubled world?

Often, love conjures thoughts of affection, romance, and sentimental expressions. But I've come to realize that it is so much more than that. I think it's time for us to redefine love. Love is not soft; love is strength. Love is not just a feeling; love is a skill, a practice to be honed. Love is most essential when it's not easy. We need love to reach beyond the happy moments. It must reach inward to ourselves and outward beyond just the people in our immediate circles to all humankind, other beings, and the earth itself.

How do we begin to practice more love? I believe the most fundamental way to love is to be fully present with your experiences, which has become a rare practice in the age of distraction and busy lifestyles. Presence with yourself begins with paying attention to your breath, your body sensations, and your emotions, without trying to change anything. Presence with others means to be fully with them, offering all of your attention with an open mind and heart. Practicing presence can be the beginning, the gateway to so many meaningful expressions of love.

Love is listening with the intent to understand, not to reply.

Love is looking into the eyes of a stranger, or simply offering a warm hello.

Love is having the compassion to remember that everyone is fighting a silent battle.

Love is accepting what is offered in the moment, without wishing it were different.

Love is noticing the veins on a leaf when the sun shines through it.

Love is having the courage to speak the truth in times of adversity, and the grace to do it peacefully.

Love is feeling sympathetic joy for the good fortune of others.

Love is pausing in gratitude for the food on our plate.

Love is forgiving. Love is apologizing.

Love is being curious about our fears and anger.

Love is watching a spider spin its web.

Love is not wasting energy blaming.

Love is allowing our vulnerability to be seen.

Love is embracing your perfectly imperfect self.

Love is finding ways to help others who are suffering.

Love is choosing to see the peace in every moment.

Love is allowing yourself to be swept away by the beauty in the world.

Love is embracing our collective humanity with people of all races, religions, and political views.

Love is appreciating our interdependence with all beings we share this beautiful planet with.

Love is a way to show up in the world every day.

Love is reminding ourselves that sometimes we fall, and we pick ourselves up and begin again.

These practices give us the power to create a better world. Rooted in love, each one draws on our innate human wisdom about what is good and right. But the stresses of life and influences of our cultures sometimes make them difficult to access. Why aren't we taught these skills in school as children? They have as much value as science, math, and languages. It is up to us to invite the cultivation of these practices into our daily lives.

Cultivating more love begins inward—practicing presence, self-compassion, patience, self-acceptance, forgiveness, trust, and gratitude with ourselves. When we learn to love ourselves more wholly, we have a greater ability to give and receive love with others. We are better able to take these practices outward to the people in our lives, such as family, friends, and colleagues. The work continues as we bring these practices of love out into our communities, where we create a ripple effect. That's the best part of love: it's contagious.

Imagine a world where we all come together with a shared commitment to more love for the collective good of humanity and the planet. When we practice looking at the world through the lens of love, we begin to see everything differently. We open ourselves up to a shift in our values; in what we consider to be essential. We change how we see each other and the earth. Only then we are empowered to advocate for a better world as voters, as consumers, as parents, as teachers, as leaders, as neighbors, and as everyday people.

Love. Could it be the answer? I believe wholeheartedly that yes, it is. With the strength of people coming together practicing its gentle power every day, we truly can make a lasting difference in the world.

Laura Murphy is the visionary behind LoveTribe, a global community that brings more understanding, loving-kindness, and mindful living into the world. She brings people together to cultivate essential simple practices that help people be gentler with themselves, each other, and the earth. Laura's passion is building community around a shared purpose to make a lasting difference in creating a kind and sustainable world. You can reach Laura at www.lovetribe.com.

Courage to Love
By McKenna Marie N.

Who would have known wanting a new bed would lead me to so many opportunities to share love and kindness?

When I was seven years old, I wanted a beautiful $750.00 Disney Princess bed. This bed wasn't just any cartoon princess bed, it was a bed made for a princess. Adorned with rose carvings, crystal ball finials, and ribbon inlay, it was simply gorgeous. When I asked my mom for this bed, she looked at the price tag and said, "If you want this bed, you're going to have to work hard and pay for it yourself."

Two and a half months later, I bought the bed with my newly-born jewelry business, called Princess Mckenna's Jewelry (PMJ). Once I accomplished that goal of buying the bed, I didn't set a new goal. The business became more of a hobby for a couple of years. I wanted to do more with my business. I just wasn't sure what direction to go.

One day my mom and I came up with an idea for an online auction concept to raise money for charity via social media. Raising money for good causes was so exciting for me! The first event, with no advertising, raised 240 dollars. We chose to work with causes that were close to my heart: foster children, animals, people with disabilities, schools, and our community. Our weekly auctions were three hours long. We sold 40 pieces of handmade jewelry each week at our peak. The production was a lot of work. This introduced us to so many amazing people, causes, experiences, and programs. When I was doing the auctions, I was able to contribute to charities and organizations that didn't recognize me as old enough to volunteer. I discovered that many people were willing and able to help me. We really created a community of love and kindness. My mom and dad helped me use the skills I had to help others and show love and kindness.

A couple of my last auctions, we raised money to help keep my school's reading program. After donating to the school, most of the kids would call me "rich" or claim that I was donating to the school for attention and likeability. They would say that my parents were the only ones donating to the school, and there weren't any auctions involved. This was ironic because, at the same time, my family was going through some tough financial times, and it was a stressful period. These auctions were a great way for us to help others and take some focus off our personal struggles. When the kids would tease me, I felt embarrassed, making me question the purpose. That, along with my school workload and age, made me feel like discontinuing the auctions.

I find myself struggling now with other kids who come from a different moral background. It's hard to find love and kindness amongst my peers. My family speaks about being an advocate for equality. I share these feelings, and it's extremely important to me. I'm scared to be myself at times, and it's hard to find courage.

I feel many of the students in school don't agree that equality for everyone is important. It's hard to find yourself when you're scared or uncomfortable to even be yourself. I remember a situation on the bus in sixth grade when a group of white students was playing border patrol, asking Hispanic students for their papers. Why would they do something like this? How do elementary school kids learn this behavior? I even feel some of the teachers might not agree with equality, so I'm not sure if I can talk to them or not. It's hard to know where in school to go, many children like myself probably feel the same. I struggle, I feel everyone in my school is divided.

While writing this, the world seems to have erupted into chaos. I've been wondering: how do you write about love in these times? Right now, it seems hard to find kindness. It's difficult for me, but it's important to talk about love right now. Even though the chaos is bringing out the worst in some, it seems to have brought out the best in others. Many people have found their voices and are starting to act. Many are taking the love movement into their own hands.

So, what do you do about the negative in the world? You need to have courage and strength in your convictions. You need to remember what love and kindness mean to you and show it at every opportunity. When you struggle as I do, you need to find people who are supportive and help you be the best you can be. Everyone learns and grows, and when you find yourself disconnected, look for groups or organizations that have similar ideas as you. Advice is hard to give, especially to myself. But what I need to remember is that I'm most likely not alone. While some things might sort themselves out, some may not, so we need to put attention on empathy and ongoing struggles. We need to put kindness first. Some things just happen, and sometimes you make it happen. When you seem surrounded by hate, that's when you need to share love the most. When I was seven years old, the love movement seemed easier, maybe we need to take a youthful approach. Bring kindness back to basics. Not everything is simple, but kindness doesn't have to be difficult.

How do I find love? I find love in being heard, spending time with those I care about, and having meaningful conversations. I know that not everyone has the same needs, so we need to listen to each other and be empathetic. We need to learn about each other, our cultures and differences. People need to be heard. We need to have our feelings validated, it doesn't take much to listen and learn if we all just try.

Mckenna Marie N. is a passionate love rebel. She is a small business owner, starting her first business endeavor at seven years old. She is a jewelry designer, poet, writer, and a student in the eighth grade.

Unchained by Shame
By Toni Lynn Pakus

I started my self-love and healing journey at the beginning of 2010. I decided I had wasted enough of my life being held captive by the secrets, lies, and denials about the abuse I endured as a child. It became essential to my sanity and mental health to be heard, be healed, and no longer bound by the trauma of my past. I had no idea the road that I was choosing would be so hollow and cold. I knew it would not be easy, but I never imagined the depths of the pit, being entangled in the vast wastelands of my mind for what seemed like an eternity. Valleys of darkness and pain, endless tears, loneliness, rejection from people I thought loved me unconditionally. Little did I know, I was never alone in my suffering. Shame blinds you to those whom God has provided to help guide you to the other side.

From the time it was reported, I was forced to pretend like my trauma did not happen the way I remembered, or that I should just let it go because others had it so much worse. For decades, this was my truth. I was not locked in a dog cage or used for satanic rituals. Many have experienced horrific circumstances that made my trauma seem insignificant. But when recently asked, "What kind of trauma is the worst kind of trauma?" I immediately answered, "Mine!" Why? Because the impact of trauma is wholly subjective and shapes how each individual interacts in the world. Many trauma survivors become advocates for human rights because they chose to find purpose in their suffering. Allowing their voices to rise out of the ashes and use it to empower others.

What will be the outcome of my suffering? I see where shame led me to choose unhealthy relationships with toxic, abusive people. I have struggled with friendships and seeing myself as someone worthy of keeping around. The lies that orbit my brain have held me in bondage for so long, it is still a daily chore to take them captive and "be transformed by the renewing of [my] mind," (Romans 12:2 NIV).

Once I could rise above the shame and see behind the lies, my decades-old filter was gone. It revealed the little girl who deserved to be held, protected, loved—not rejected or abandoned—accepted and cherished. At the beginning of 2020, during my prayer time, I asked God to show me His purpose and His plan in this new decade. While my cousin and I were praying together, she said, "No, Tone! It's a new era, not a new decade! God is ushering in a new era, and the things that normally take years will take days, things that take decades will take months." A new fire ignited in my spirit, revealing to me a new future of possibilities: I could see it, feel it, and taste it. I am blameless, shameless, no longer broken inside. It was going to happen; it was no longer just a cry to God, waiting for an answer. It was coming. It was here, and it would shine like a light to guide others out of their darkness.

I spent several months writing a poem about shame, and now I see that through the filter of shame, I was cut off from being able to love myself and others while embodying my worth and value. I raised two amazing children into adulthood while living through the filter of shame. I love them both with my entire being, but did they pay the cost? *See, the lies they still creep in sometimes, but I always have an answer!*

LIE: Do they know even in the slightest that I would lay my life down for them in an instant?

ANSWER: Of course, they do!

LIE: Did I really do my best to be a loving and nurturing mother, even in the prison of my shame and worthlessness?

ANSWER: Hell yes!

LIE: Do they see the world with wounded spirits and brokenness, or are they strong and determined to rise above the trials they will face?

ANSWER: Maybe, but I pray, "Lord, may they see the power of perseverance, prayer, and how you are ever-present in their time of trouble. In Jesus' name, Amen!"

This has been an arduous journey, and I can honestly say I have felt lost so many times along the way. I see now that each moment was held by God to use for His ultimate glory. I was provided for, supported, and loved—sometimes despite myself. He has led me to break free from shame's hold. I see my life full of limitless possibilities, limitless faith, unchained by the prison of my shame. I am free to love myself and others unconditionally and know this is the mark of my freedom! By the blood of the cross, I am set free. I am free, indeed.

Shame

It... lies

It... haunts

It... torments

It... taunts

It... imprisons a multitude

It... steals from the heart of you

It... corrodes the spirit

It... reveals to you your deepest fears

It... makes itself high priest

It... masquerades itself as pride

It... pretends to be your armor and shield

It... seems the safest place to hide

It acts a lot like fear you see, this shame that bleeds you dry. The only way to ever be free, is to shake free of the lie

The chains they weigh so heavy now, they keep your spirit bound

Your shackles: once your protective shield, keep you from Heaven's crown

Shame will keep you from the joy of your heart, all that makes life worthwhile

So, release them for your freedom my dear, freedom for God's little child

We all have purpose in suffering when we hide behind shame no more

When the chains are gone let your light shine free and delight thee in the Lord.

Toni Lynn Pakus is a trauma coach, nontoxic living expert, and love rebel. She helps women find their voice in the midst of their darkness and isolation to empower them to rise from the ashes and see the world with limitless faith, knowing that they are supported, loved, and on their path to true healing. Her passion is to help you remove the toxins from all areas of your life: mind, body and spirit so you can protect your family from repeating the same patterns. You can reach Toni at toni@puretoni.com.

Remembering Katrina
By Toni Lynn Pakus

O n April 22, 2016, eight months after Hurricane Katrina, I boarded an airplane heading to St. Bernard Parish, one of the areas most devastated, with five of my friends from church. Although we were not friends before this trip—I did not know any of them—by the end, we were bound together for eternity. Just as one of these trips might do to a group of people. On the flight there and the flight home, I wrote a little bit that I feel could bring some light into the world today.

It was not a fun vacation, it was a necessary one and one that changed my entire trajectory. Instead of writing a lot about the trip, I'm just going to share a couple of poems that tell the story. If you can read this poem in light of what's happening in the world right now—2020— pandemic, economy, civic unrest, injustices all around. If you happen to be safe in your little bubble or maybe feel that you just are not seen, I see you. I feel you. I hear you. I love you. You are not alone.

Journal entry: Great is the Lord 4/22/2006

Your power and wisdom are beyond our imagination. You set forth a path for the adventures that lie ahead. We go into this unknowing what you have in store. We just believe it is for your glory and to further your kingdom, and we gladly fold and bend to be utilized in ways we may never understand. We can be certain that eternity will show just what effect we've had. I know that each of us is excited to not only see the benefits when we enter your kingdom, but whole-heartedly we look forward to the labor and work you will have us do. To help save someone's home from having to be completely demolished or just to find some of the keepsakes they long to hold on to for a memory of their life, work, or family history.

A Prelude to Serve

Your purposes unknown when your mighty wrath reigns down.

Hearts and lives are broken when it claims a state or town.

Everything lost in the twinkle of an eye.

A terrible storm comes, and it flies right by.

Wrecking and ravaging everything in its path.

The floodwaters rise after the blast.

People left homeless, loved ones are gone.

Some passed on after the storm, some left all alone.

Although we don't know if you always have a plan.

You lift people up to lend a helping hand.

When all hope is lost, you show your loving care.

You send out your people.

You take them right there.

To the most devastated of places.

Where no one will go.

To tear through the ruble and show signs of some hope.

You bring there your people, and gladly they come.

By hundreds and hundreds to help the old and the young.

This is a purpose we cannot understand.

But it's not up to us to know your perfect plan.

You are always good at whatever you do.

And those we have lost—we pray they're with you.

So guide our way, Lord, in every little step.

And prepare our hearts to cherish every single breath.

The day will soon come when we'll look upon your face.

And thank you, Lord Jesus, for your saving grace.

4/29/06 The Aftermath

Feeling numb.

Can't explain it.

All the pictures.

They can't contain it.

The vast destruction for miles and miles.

On a few faces, you see a few smiles.

Some still angry for all that they lost.

What a price to pay—just count the cost.

Thousands of people have lost their homes.

Will they be rebuilt or forever have to roam.

Not quite sure what will happen next.

Where will they go to just find some rest?

Love Meets Life

Still waiting for trailers and houses need gutting.

Some to be demolished, but their lawns they keep cutting.

Planting fresh flowers repairing wounded trees.

Just trying to bring life back to their communities.

They are so tight these neighbors in Chalmette.

We can't just go home and let ourselves forget.

We went and did God's work; we couldn't sit and stare.

At night we got back to rest—we'd have prayer time and share.

Share about the reality that no one else can know.

You must see with your own eyes what the pictures can't show.

The pain and the heartache still lingers and reigns.

But the hope we can bring them will lessen their pains.

Until you get in there and reach out to the folks.

The houses you're cleaning—the lives you give hope.

They tell you all about it—the flood as it came.

The winds as they whistled didn't bring all the pain.

The water rush in a foot every minute.

They ran to the attic, shoved everyone in it.

Sawing the roof and hacking away.

They had to get through it for the hope of escape.

Nowhere to run.

Love Meets Life

Nowhere to hide.

They just had to hold on to this horrible ride.

Some houses shook. Some swept right away.

Others moved inches and now rot in decay.

They say there for days. Six to be exact.

No one was allowed in; they all were sent back.

Some decided they just could not wait.

Loved ones needed them—some were too late.

Some had to make choices they find hard to let go of.

One man tried his hardest as the waters continued to flow.

It's not about the storm that wiped out this place.

It's about the hearts who lived there and their desire to see God's face.

Their faith in Him stronger than ever before.

Unwilling to be frozen by fear anymore.

They are strong and courageous; they won't be knocked down.

They continue to fight because Jesus wears His crown.

May you remember this one day when you feel alone.

May you remember Katrina and find your way home.

Toni Lynn Pakus is a trauma coach, nontoxic-living expert, and love rebel. She helps women find their voice in the midst of their darkness and isolation to empower them to rise from the ashes and see the world with limitless faith, knowing that they are supported, loved, and on their path to true healing. Her passion is to help you remove the toxins from all areas of your life: mind, body, spirit—so you can protect your family from repeating the same patterns. You can reach Toni at toni@puretoni.com.

The Making Of Universal Love
By Shannon Phillips

When we're young, we are taught a host of things, pieces that shape the adults we turn into. The inner workings of our being slowly began to be built by the hands of those around us. In my parents' hands, they held paintbrushes that dripped vibrant colors. Pink, yellow, blue, orange, red, and purple hues worked their way into crafting me. They molded me with the perfect mix of calm and chaos—my mother being a peaceful, reserved, strong intellect, and my father being a vibrant, daring, outgoing spirit. One thing that stuck to my memory and clung to my being was family gatherings.

No matter if it were my in-state family, my brothers' friends, my friends, out of state family, or my parents' friends, they knew how to hold a get-together. One of the things that I remember is my father's family's fish fries.

My father grew up in Arkansas, a country state that values family. My family threw some of the biggest fish fries I've seen. From my eyes as a child growing into a teenager, I saw and felt so many good vibes. The setting was always filled with love. The smell of fish would always fill my nose and make my mouth water. Sometimes they caught the fish we ate, sometimes they bought it, and sometimes a mix of the two. My dad liked to man the fish fryer with a cousin or two. Talking of how they could fry the best fish and who had the best coating mix, either way, it was exceptional to taste on your tongue.

The adults would play cards. If you know anything about spades, you know it's a challenging number game. Four players, two sets of partners, and your partner better know how to play. Call your books right, or there'll be a lot of stare downs at the table. It gets pretty intense, and you'll hear yelling from time to time. I didn't learn how to play until I was 14. There were groups of people everywhere: adults, teenagers, kids, and mixes of the three. These fish fries weren't just for family, but for the entire city. Everyone knew our family, and we knew them. As long as you had positivity and love, you could come to hang out. The gathering was filled with good conversation, games, laughs, and dancing. These fish fries let me know a few things; food, good drinks, family, and love made for a great time.

I took my family's gatherings and inserted them into my own lifestyle, really young. My parents allowed me to throw myself parties when I hit 16, I would think of a million things to include to have a good time. Water balloon fights, game nights, anything that brought a group of people together for a good time. Food was always a huge element. I'd have my dad fry fish, BBQ, or I'd cook—taco bars, pasta, chips and dip, anything that could fill a ton of bellies. Music was also a key element; a speaker could always be found playing the hottest music. We'd always dance, because dancing never gets old.

Around this time, I was also introduced to events by key leaders in my community. This inserted another element into gatherings, and my teenage mind exploded with possibilities. I saw many ways to create different experiences for different reasons. Whether I was helping with an event at school, my church, my dance school, or my boyfriend's mom, I'd be involved. I helped with artistic events, tea parties, ceremonies, award shows, galas, performances, meetings, training, workshops, birthday parties—gatherings of all sorts. I just wanted to be around people. People gathering in love, knowledge, and positivity.

I continued my gatherings into college with my husband. With him being a football player and me being in the art world, we were never short of good people. We would BBQ every weekend it seemed. Food, good company, drinks, games, and music filled our space.

When we moved to Arizona, I decided I would hop into the event planning world. I was tired of assisting with community events. I wanted to create my own experiences for people. I wanted to highlight amazing individuals in the community. I wanted to spread love in the manner I knew how—gatherings! I first started with modeling workshops, going back home to coach women and girls about the modeling industry, and giving them the tools they needed to be successful and jump-start their journey. I wanted to directly help the city that gave me so many good memories. Davenport, Iowa, is a smaller city, but it gave me so many important elements. The city really aided my artistic side and pushed me to want more.

In 2019, I had the opportunity to create an event with the Tempe Center for the Arts. I was thrilled beyond explanation. The leader of the program gave me free rein to create an event however I wanted. I instantly knew I wanted to bring a lot of people together with love as the message. From this, Universal Love was created. The message is simple: love. I used pink as the main color, pink is the color of universal love of oneself and of others. Working in the art and fashion community, I wanted to bring us together in collaboration and love. The event is a multidisciplinary performance that sheds light on artists and businesses in the Arizona community and spreads positive energy to every participant. Participants and artists are urged to dress up in pink, as dressing up helps with confidence. It also gives the fashion community a chance to do what they do best, dress to impress! We included food and drink elements to aid the flow of the evening—DJs to fill the space with good music during networking periods. We also inserted feel-good moments like photo booths, love jars (a chance to write a positive message to someone that will be read during the event), and interactive art displays. Helping with the dialogue of love starts with you. Spreading love can be simple if you let it. This is what fueled me to start Universal Love. I'm one person, but my actions can affect hundreds of people. If I must leave a mark, it has to be positive.

All of my life, I was blessed to be surrounded by people who loved what they did. My family and their gatherings, my dance instructors, my teachers, my mother-in-law, and so many other people. When I grew older, I filled my surroundings with artistic people who would go to the end of the world for their crafts. I've seen people go the extra mile for art and their passions, me included. I wanted to make those people feel valued and let them know we *see* you. When I figured out I could take what I loved from my youth and intertwine it with my adult life, I knew I found a golden key. Bringing the community together in the name of love fills my heart with so much joy. To let people glow in their unapologetic light is beautiful to witness.

I'm honored to be able to continue Universal Love. The response from the community was so huge I'm now able to create multiple events that shine a light on talented members of our community. I figured out a way to put everything I love into an event while aiding my true purpose; spreading love. My need to create loving environments, spaces that are open, and non-judgmental safe havens, in celebration of people, have been fulfilled. Love truly starts with you, and if authentic, spreads like wildfire. I challenge you to find what you love and do it unapologetically with love in your heart. Spread love always and find your light. Someone is waiting for your glow to spark theirs!

Shannon Love Phillips is a native of Iowa. She's a fashion model, dancer, choreographer, influencer, social media guru, and photographer.

Shannon's experiences led her to partner with reputable community leaders and brands. With the community's support, she's held workshops, events, and speaking engagements for the betterment and direct needs of all artists. With education and support, she found "keys" that helped her enter unheard of doors. She strives to give out these keys by educating her following and offering them the love, knowledge, and support it takes to succeed. As she continues to grow and learn, she hopes to inspire people to live their dreams. Shannon can be reached at ShannonLoveBookings@gmail.com or via Instagram: @UniversalLoveEvents or @TheRealShannonLove.

Things My Mother Taught Me
By Demetra Presley

A s a child, my mother taught me to love reading and the joy that comes from getting lost in a good book. That even though I did not like math, I still had to learn how to do it. That there was more to doing laundry then simply putting clothes in the washer—I had to add detergent to the water too. To never let the world tell me who I was. To eat the little pieces of breaded fish left in the frying pan because they are delicious. Yes, pajamas are Christmas gifts. Playing the trombone was going to take some practice. If I wanted to go somewhere with her, I better be ready on time or move fast enough to catch the car before she pulled out of the driveway. Graduating high school and going to college were not options, but expectations. One day when the glasses came off, and the braces were gone, I would be able to see what she always did. A bad day could always be made better by taking a bubble bath. The family was everything, and I was to always look out for my brother. There was something about eating junk food in secret that made it taste better. She wasn't kidding when she said she was going to chaperone my junior prom. To give, and to do so graciously, because it was the right thing to do.

As an adult, my mother taught me she would answer my call no matter how late at night or early in the morning it was. She was absolutely correct in not giving me the recipe for her pie because she knew when left unsupervised, I would eat an entire one by myself. To not let something that appeared hard, prevent me from doing it anyway. She knew exactly how long the drive was between Tucson, Arizona, and Phoenix and could figure out how fast I was going by how quickly I arrived home. Yes, even after you turned 18, you could still receive pajamas as Christmas gifts. No, me having a deep fryer was probably not the best idea. To not let another person define what I could or could not accomplish. Bubble baths still made the day better, even more so when a glass of wine was added. The importance of finding a good hairstylist who knew how to properly care for my hair. To not compromise or settle for less than what I really wanted. There was no age limit to telling on my brother to get him in trouble. When I came home and wanted to take food back with me, to either return her plastic containers or make do with Ziploc bags because she was not giving me anymore of her Tupperware. She was wrong about me not being able to pull off the color red. She could nurse anything back to health, including my sick pet fish. Make the choices that I believed were the best for me. There was still no place like home.

On April 2, 2011, the morning my mother died, she taught me heartbreak. She taught me the sorrow that comes from watching the body of the person who loved and cared for you your entire life, slowly begin its escape from pain, to finally rest. She taught me no matter how hard you pray or how many times you wish, sometimes those prayers and wishes will go unanswered. She taught me even though your world might feel like it is ending, it will indeed begin again, anew, the next morning. She taught me to continue breathing, even if every inhale and exhale hurt. She taught me the comfort that comes from memories. She taught me how lucky I was to have had someone in my life whose absence would be felt so deeply. She taught me grief was the price that is paid for love. She taught me there was some heartache you did not get over or move on from, but that you simply learned to live with and carry. She taught me the best way to honor someone was to be the things you loved the most about them.

My mother still teaches me. When I look in the mirror and see the brown skin and brown eyes that resemble hers, she teaches me to love the body I occupy and the strength, life, and breath, it holds. When I reach the final page of a good book, she teaches me the strength of words and to use my own to create magic, educate, inspire, and uplift others. When I see photographs of us together, she teaches me to stay in the moment that I am in, to be present and feel all that it carries, because time is fleeting. When I see the degrees hanging on my walls, she teaches me that education and learning is a lifelong process and to strive to grow and become more. When I enter the office of my non-profit organization, she teaches me service, because giving is always the right thing to do. When I see my father, she teaches me to love and to seek a life partner that will, in the moments of my last breath, be there holding my hand.

Above all us, my mother taught me to love. Love that was deep, self-sacrificing, and abundant, with no limits. Love that supported and cheered for every accomplishment and picked me up and propelled me forward when I stumbled and fell. Love that showed me how to navigate the world with strength and resiliency. Love that taught me how to care about other people, whether they were family and friends, or complete strangers. Love that encouraged hard work and perseverance. Love that gave me the ability to create my path and stand in my own power. My mother taught me the most valuable lesson to be learned, one that could only be demonstrated through an example: unconditional, powerful, generous, unfaltering, love.

Demetra Presley is Executive Director of Go With The Flow, a non-profit organization based in Arizona that provides menstrual supplies to students and low income and homeless community members in Arizona. She graduated from Arizona State University with a Bachelor of Science and Masters of Science in Justice Studies. She has over ten years of experience working in social services and is passionate about women's reproductive healthcare and menstrual equity.

You can reach Demetra at www.gowiththeflowaz.org or gowiththeflowaz@gmail.com.

Soul Alchemy
By Kim Purcell

What if you could change your life for the better? I mean, soul-deep. Make your children thrive, all your relationships better, and boost your happiness quotient. You can transform your lineage for generations to come, releasing ancestral trauma embedded in your cells. Would you do it? I know it's a lofty claim. But it's guaranteed! And it's free!

Have you ever been so in love, you felt light and airy like you had wings? Alchemy is a seemingly supernatural process of transformation. And so it is with love. Love transforms. When we reopen to love, we connect soul-deep, and the ripple effect is felt generationally: past, present, and future. Now stay with me. We 'send good vibes,' and '*feel* the love.' It's an energetic vibration. There are different emotional frequencies like there are different stations on the radio. When we are in love, we are at the top of the scale, closest to Heaven. The power of love harnesses the power of the divine.

It's not always Abracadabra! Poof! We go from unloved to overflowing love in an instant—bam! But it is possible if you're willing to do the work. I spent a lifetime feeling unloved. Whether true or only true to me, the dark cloak weighed on my soul for a long time. When I began to do soul work, I never imagined what would become available all in one magical moment. I've come to learn what hit me like a tsunami can whisper to us all in different ways. Subtle or intense, the transformative power of love does not discriminate. We are infinitely more powerful than we've ever been taught.

When our hearts are pure, our energies are clear. We emit more vibrantly, like a beacon with a clean lens. Imagine the lens is cracked; the tunnel of light that shines is broken or blurred. Emotional bloat weighs down our souls and muddies our chance to shine.

When I re-awoke to love, heart shapes showered from nature, like a hailstorm. They came from every crevice in the universe to get the divine message across: rocks, leaves, clouds, gum spots on the sidewalk. Finally, I see. It's me. Everything we see is a reflection of ourselves, a projection of our own unique energetic blueprint at that moment in time. I became so immersed in love; it was echoing back to me. For a time, I minimized it as simply a knack for finding the shape, like shark's teeth in the sand. But that doesn't give soul work its due credit.

To open our hearts, we must clear away calcification that accumulates each time we believe we are unloved. We build walls. I invite you to crack open that chrysalis that has formed around your heart and see the majestic grace and wisdom that love has to teach us. Give love back its wings, and watch it expand and transform your life.

Sound works wonders. Tink a wine glass and hear a high-pitched ping. Ping a frequency high enough and shatter the glass. So it follows sound can demolish the fortress around your heart. It's not voodoo science; it's vibration.

Remember, sound waves are vibration. Try humming with the intention to clear your soul. Exhale and release an audible hum. Hit different notes and feel the hum resonate differently throughout your body, from your belly to the tips of your temples. Feel it. Hum head to toe, inviting divine love magic to flow unhindered throughout your entire mind, body, and soul. You are your own healer. We *allow* ourselves to be closed to love or open to a heavenly expansion of our souls. In love, everyone and everything is just a little bit delicious. I invite you to *savor some scrumption* and let your heart sing like a child again, unafraid and free. Remember, those walls weren't built in a day. Give yourself time with this decalcification practice.

Become your own soul alchemist, using this process I created, called HEART.

H - Heal old wounds. Acknowledge what shaped the way you love. Doing so in the third person can help, as you emotionally detach from your timeline of love. Recognize those events are part of your story. They are not *you*. Put those events in their place in the past.

E - Erase emotional bloat. Release negative, heavy energies from the body. Center. Breathe. Release. Notice where each emotion resides in your body. Hum directly into that space and let it go. Imagine retiring each emotion on a raft, setting it free on a wave. Release each emotion, good, bad, and ugly. Break your emotional attachment to your past stories. Depending on the density of your trauma, you may need help with this part.

A – Awareness. Become the witness to ways you give and want to receive love. Become present to your own love story without judgment of others or yourself.

R - Reframe, refocus, revise. Identify the times you chose to believe you were not worthy of love. Question: Are they really true?

T - Transform and Thrive. Allow yourself to experience love and see your soul shine.

Practice reconnecting with HEART in relationships too. Witness yourself in a relationship. Are you consistently taking on a role? Victim, servant, the knight in shining armor, emotionally unavailable. Notice how you give and receive love. Be kind and gentle with yourself. Release any heavy energies in each relationship, like resentment, jealousy, anger, etc. Notice them. Acknowledge them and let them go. If there are wounds to heal, identify what it will take to heal those relationships, or let them go. Forgive, apologize, do what it takes to have peace in your soul. There's no promise of tomorrow. Clear the air. Become *present* in the relationship.

Love is magic. Fear tells us to hoard our love and that we'll become depleted. But love has different alchemy altogether. The more you give, the more you're nourished by it. How magical is that!? Is there anything else in the world that the more we give away, the more gushes in?

Love and generosity are on the same frequency. When we feel loved, we learn to love others again, freely and fully.

Kim Purcell is a wellness workshop facilitator and self-love coach. Married for 19 years, she and her husband have three thriving teenagers. Kim worked in publishing for 15 years, where she developed her passion for nutrition. Diagnosed with Crohn's/Colitis, Kim healed herself through food and nutrition. Her passion for healing the body is rivaled only by a passion for healing the whole soul self. For the past 7 years, Kim has been working with women and teen girls on their journeys toward mind, body, and spiritual wellness in Ponte Vedra Beach, Florida. She loves to help in any way she can.

Find her on Facebook as Kim Droge Purcell or www.facebook.com/thrivetribekp or email agehealthier@gmail.com or call (904) 545-1327.

Learning Self-Love Through The Gift Of Surrogacy
By Carly Rebuck

"Her HCG levels have risen. They are not quite where we want them to be, but they have risen, and we can confirm that the implantation was successful."

As I hung up the phone with the news that our surrogate was pregnant, I had tears in my eyes as I turned to my brother, who that day had become my business partner through the purchase and stock transfer of a family business, and uttered the words to him that it finally took. Our surrogate was pregnant with his niece or nephew. He cried as I hastily called my husband with the news and then called and cried with our surrogate. This was a big day, a life-changing day. I would not have imagined six years earlier everything that was happening in April of 2018.

When I met my first husband at twenty-four, and he explained that he did not want children because of a genetic condition that ran in his family, I agreed. At thirty-one when our divorce was finalized, I had hope for the first time that having a child was now a possibility for me.

A year after I separated and six months after the divorce was finalized, I decided that I was ready to start dating again. For the first time in ten years. In the age of internet dating. I posted a single picture on a dating website and answered questions honestly on a Thursday night and had my first date on Saturday morning to meet a man eleven years my senior for breakfast pancakes. We married seventeen months later.

Neither my second husband nor I had children from previous marriages, and we wanted to try together. Infertility followed with bad news at every appointment... low sperm counts, no ovulation, direct to IVF, shots, tests, blood draws, and endless ultrasounds. Being pregnant with twins at Christmas and losing one right after the holiday and the other right after the new year created a sense of longing at every holiday after that. A singleton was next and was lost as well. Further bad news, more doctors, and flights around the country eventually led to a determination that my uterus was incapable of holding life.

My husband held my hand throughout. He supported every decision I wanted to make and shockingly found a co-worker and friend's wife in the non-surrogacy-friendly State of Arizona to help us have our child. The first night I met our surrogate was the night we discussed her carrying our final quality embryo. She gave freely and without reservation her love, care, and support for our decision. She gave us hope.

Months of preparation followed, and implantation occurred. I heard the fateful words; her levels are rising, and she is pregnant. I sat next to her, and we watched as the doctor used an instrument that released the embryo inside her womb. I sat next to her as she offered us the most precious gift while I was holding her hand. I could not put our surrogate in a bubble or a clean room, and watching her drive away that first day was heart-wrenching. I could not control anything she did, or anywhere she went, and that was my first experience of being a parent. Being a parent is about letting go, trusting, trying, worrying, and trusting some more.

The embryo decided not to stay. The first time our surrogate had had a miscarriage after five successful pregnancies and children with her husband. An experience she went through because of her love and hope for us. This was our last chance and hope for parenthood. Well-meaning friends and family mentioned fostering, mentioned adoption, but after years of the ups and downs of infertility and loss, taking either of those steps felt too emotional for either of us to handle. We accepted that there had to be more, and we searched for what that more was.

In my search for more, I found myself. I looked in the mirror each morning and realized the person I needed to love and accept was staring back at me. So much is said about being unable to love others until you have loved yourself, and if you cannot love yourself, what are you to anyone else? I had always considered these sayings trite. I had married my first husband at the blessing of my parents and family, whose name looked beautiful on a wedding invitation, in a perfect ceremony through the Catholic Church and reception in my parent's backyard. My second marriage was all mine, with a joyful ceremony in the tunnel of love in Las Vegas married with Elvis singing to us by a pastor with beautiful dreadlocks. Our infertility story was a part of who we are. It brought us closer, showed us love, but ended without our wish for a child.

I needed a purpose, I needed to do, I needed more, and I had the strength to express this to those around me. To express to my business partner and brother that the company was not enough. To express to my husband, who I loved dearly, that he was also not enough. That I needed to find me. I had put so much into my first marriage, family business and infertility struggles that I had lost sight of who I was. I found myself realizing that one person can make a difference, that one person can fashion a world that they see through rose-colored and heart-shaped glasses and change that world into something better by finding their tribe of like-minded women and men who also strive towards hope, light, and love.

Carly C. Rebuck is co-owner with her brother of MPB Realty Services, Inc., a second-generation company that provides commercial property management, leasing, and brokerage services to building owners and their tenants. Carly lives in Phoenix with her husband and six rescued senior dogs. She is privileged to speak out about her infertility experiences to show others struggling that they are not alone. She is emboldened through the support of powerful women leaders to lend her voice and financial support to charities, political organizations, and candidates she believes in. She urges everyone to vote so that their voices can be heard and counted.

Sacrifice For Love
By Sandy Rogers

The year was 1963; I had just turned 15 in June. The new school year was in full swing in the small town in Ohio, where I lived with my mother, father, and three younger siblings. I had been attending this school since kindergarten.

I was now a sophomore in high school with a class size of fewer than 100 students. In those days, there were the popular girls who were smart or cheerleaders, or they were on the drill team, or were just the pretty girls.

I was not one of them. I was just barely five feet tall, with unruly brown hair, and was painfully shy. When I was three years old, I started dance classes, and dance had been a creative outlet for me. When the opportunity came to try out for the drill team, I took it. When I got chosen to be on the drill team, it put me in the "in-crowd." Dancing was something that I felt good at, and being on the drill team allowed me to express that while performing at the football games. Being on the drill team gave me a sense of accomplishment and acceptance.

That year, a new boy enrolled in school. Although, he was somewhat of a mystery because he never really shared with anyone why his family had moved to town from Kentucky. He was good-looking, tall, with curly blond hair and blue eyes. He quickly became a part of the in-crowd as well as the object of attention with the popular girls.

The fall dance was coming up in October. I had never had a date. So, when the new boy asked me if I wanted to go to the dance, I was beyond surprised. He was a year older than me and was already driving. To my surprise, when I asked my parents if I could go, they said yes.

On the Saturday night of the dance, he picked me up at my home. Of course, he had to come to the door so that both my parents could meet him to "give their approval."

I now understood what the term "giddy like a schoolgirl" meant. My stomach was churning with excitement as we entered the gymnasium at the school decorated in brilliant fall colors. And, when the popular girls saw me walk in with him, they were visibly surprised. We had a wonderful evening, and I was dancing on cloud nine.

He drove me home and, to my surprise, he wanted to kiss me. Well, that kiss led to more kissing, which led to making out, which led to "doing it." I didn't know I was doing anything wrong!

Yes, first date, first kiss, and first time doing it! Looking back, I now know that my mother never gave me the "talk." You know, the one about sex and how you get pregnant.

Six weeks pass by, and he and I have had a few other dates. We are now into Christmas break from school. It is the Sunday after Christmas, and my mother asks me if I have let him touch me? I ask her what she means, and she then explains in detail. She realized that I had not had my period. My mother became enraged—at me! "How could you do that?" she yelled.

The next thing I knew, she had called our family doctor at home. He told her to bring me to his office, and he would meet us there so he could examine me. I had never had "that" exam before and didn't know what was happening.

After the exam, he told her I was about six weeks pregnant. I don't remember a lot of what happened after that. I do remember my mother was furious at me.

When we arrived back home, she and my father sat down with me, and they decided that the boy and I had to get married because they did not want an illegitimate grandchild. Their anger, again at me, was frightening.

The decision made by my parents and the boy's parents was that we would go to the county courthouse and be married by a judge. There was no wedding.

We went back to school on a Monday after Christmas break, and on Tuesday, my parents, the boy's parents, and he and I all went to the county courthouse. The marriage performed now ensured this baby would be legitimate.

I went back to school the next day and called to the Principal's office. He asked two questions: "Are you pregnant?" and "Did you get married yesterday?" Of course, I answered honestly. He then said that I had to leave school immediately. Remember, this was now January 1964. Things were very different back then, especially in small-town America.

I never saw the boy after that.

The choice my parents gave me was that if I kept the baby, it would not be my child, but brought up as my brother or sister. Somehow, I knew I was unable to do that.

Ironically, my parents put me in a home for unwed mothers (I was legally married). This place was like a prison. As an example, the only phone we were given access to was a wooden phone booth that was chained and padlocked after 6:00 pm every night.

Because of the decision to either give up or keep my baby, manipulated by my parents' demand, I chose to give up, what would become my only child. The ultimate sacrifice of love is to surrender your child.

I never knew if I had a boy or a girl. My decision, the only one I was allowed to make, was that if I was to surrender my child to adoption, that I could not see or know the gender of my child. It would be the hardest decision of my life. At 27, I learned I had a son.

Surrendering my son was the real sacrifice for love.

Her peers know Sandy Rogers in the holistic, spiritual, and metaphysical business arena as the Referral Queen. She promotes businesses, events, and products via: AskSandyRogers.com eAnnouncement service.

Also, she is a birthmother who surrendered her only child to adoption. An advocate for adoption reform in 1987, helped create new law in Kentucky that allowed adult adoptees to petition the courts for their original birth certificates. In 2020, she testified in the Arizona Legislature for similar law changes. Sandy holds the copyright to the book, *The 5 Year Journal* (The5YearJournal.com).

You can learn more at AskSandyRogers.com or email Sandy@AskSandyRogers.com.

You Came To Love
By Raelin Saindon

"You came to love, to be love, you are love."
- Raelin Saindon

These words moved through me smoothly, and with a flow of truth, I can only explain the event as a divine proclamation powerfully spoken upon his life and its purpose in that immediate moment. Sitting across from me was this beautiful young man, wide-eyed at being witnessed so completely by a stranger, and finally able to breathe deeply for the first time in his memory to that point. He has lived with such turmoil, rejection, and mixed messages from so many adults in his young walk upon this earth. I watched his body melt as those words were received by his soul, drinking them up as parched earth opens up to the rain, soaking it in and being satiated after a long drought. We both just sat there staring, hearing what each other's eyes were speaking. I'll never forget it.

I have been called in this life to witness the lives of others. I guess you could say I'm an observer, but there's so much more to it than that. I see, hear, know, and listen to what people are sharing about their inner world in every exchange that I have. It's not something that I can "turn off" or wish away, and I dare say that we are all wired with this same "being-ness." We all operate based upon energy; emotions are defined as 'energy-in-motion,' and it is how we navigate the world around us. It is pure awareness and focused attention or intention that sets some individuals apart in these abilities.

My earliest memories of knowing things about people and my environment, all had to do with feeling my way into situations that I watched going on with other people. Arguments, disagreements, and even happy moments were all spoken to me through the lens of love. If I saw or heard a playground fight or someone being picked upon, I would be there to defend or to try to get both parties to see one another instead of furthering the divide. I have always been led with this desire for people to see and honor each other for whom and what they are at the soul-level and find the love that exists within each of them in that space.

Love in the English language has been sterilized and confused with over-use. We "love" hotdogs, apple pie, brand name clothes, sports teams, celebrities, television shows, and anything else pop-culture feeds us. We've lost the full weight of its meaning and transformative power-until we see or experience miracle moments of profound humanity through even the simplest of kindnesses.

Love takes on many forms, some that even challenge our narrow definitions. Pain is felt when caring for an open wound, but love is there. Anguish is felt at the loss of someone dear, but love is there. Suffering cries out for relief and ending, but love is there.

Love is in every social situation, event, upset, and celebration. It's up to us to focus our lens.

A sacred aspect of love is the willingness to bear witness. We largely know this as the act of testifying to the truth, evidence seen, heard, or lived. What I'm speaking of takes it deeper. It is the powerful act of love being demonstrated when we can sit with another and simply honor them as they are, where they are, and the totality that has shaped them without judgment or urges to fix. Being so centered in the knowledge that we are not here to *dictate* the work of experiencing life and healing that each soul has come to step into for them, we can then compassionately *see* them. Witness the upsets, the challenges, the tragedies, the celebrations, the overcoming, that each human being walks within this lifetime. Through all of that, we gain clarity of their inhabitation and unique relationship with love.

Love, just like light, holds contrasts within it. I mentioned some previously, and it bears repeating. Even the lives of individuals that act in ways so defiling, bankrupt, and we would categorize as "no respecter of life," point us toward love. The backdrop of their behaviors and experiences can be as close to the darkest shade of black we might imagine, and yet if we settle in, we can see and hear love along the way. The violations of love's presence. The affront to love's compassionate offers. The rejection of love's healing power. The denial of love's reality. The refusal to heed love's calls.

There exists no place, no time, no distance, no event, and no experience where love is not there. When we allow honest reflection of our darkest periods of life, we can see the threads that love weaves alongside the pain, loss, grief, and tragedy. If we attempt to pull on the strings, we would rather not see or feel, we unravel the entire tapestry and love's presence as well. How then can we reconcile these contrasts, these opposing forces at work among humanity?

I look to nature and its honest teachings it has for us. The earth cannot support plants, forests, and grasses without the ground being broken open, disrupted, and overturned. Seeds cannot bear fruit or bloom without being buried deeply, broken open, and disintegrated so the plant within can erupt through the earth and grow tall and strong. Leaves of trees provide shade, nourishment, and cover and yet are naturally shed in due time so they can be consumed by the earth once again to feed the life within it. Creation springs from destruction and destruction supports new life. There is no separation between these two, except the perception that we hold about them as opposites. In reality, it is all the same process. Love is of that same reality as well.

You came to love.

You came to be love.

You are love.

In every word, thought, and deed, let us *be* one with love.

Raelin Saindon calls herself an "Observer & Advocate" of humanity and The Soul that lives within others. She operates as a Healing Channel of WE are WE Consciousness and her business, The Healing Space. She is also a Best-selling Author of "The Ultimate Guide to Self-Healing Techniques."

Raelin uses her training in energy modalities such as Reiki and Hypnosis, psychology, and storytelling to empower others through inquiry and "Live the Softer Way."

She hosts a weekly podcast, "Live OUT LOUD" at
www.anchor.fm/raelin-saindon
You can connect with her on her website at
www.raelinsaindon.com
FB: www.facebook.com/thehealingspaceco/
Instagram: www.instagram.com/thehealingspaceco/
YouTube: https://bit.ly/3fECgMM

Stepping Into Self-Love
By Megan Sampson

I vividly remember how distraught I felt while sitting on my couch in March 2008, looking like a total cliché crying and eating ice cream while flipping through the pages of a magazine thinking, "I wish that was me." After two failed relationships and two devastating miscarriages, I felt unattached, unworthy, and unloved. "I'm not good enough" had become the core belief in my life. I had stopped going out and started eating my feelings. I stopped weighing myself when I saw "299.2" on the scale because I knew I wouldn't be able to process knowing that I was over 300 pounds. I was in the deepest part of my depression, and I didn't know how to get out of it.

And then I turned the page in the magazine…

Learn to walk a marathon or half marathon!

I don't know what spiritually happened to me at that moment, but instantly I said out loud, "That's it. That is what I am going to do." Within a week, I was signed up for the Long Beach Half Marathon in October of that year. That gave me over six months to train for this thing. Six months to focus on something else besides being depressed.

I bought my first pair of sneakers and decided to hit the pavement. "Look at that! I am out of the house!" Thankfully my neighborhood had the perfect two-mile loop that was very walker-friendly. I would walk 2-6 miles every day. Then the Arizona summer heat hit. I could not deal with the amount of heat at all hours of the day, and I stopped training. It sounds sad, but I have learned that I am very grateful for that period of "giving up" because it was in those three months that I learned a very valuable lesson: I missed walking.

It took me those three months to realize that I wasn't just training for a race. I wasn't just walking to walk. I realized that in each walk, I got to quiet my mind for as long as I wanted. In each walk, I got to know a little bit more about myself. In each walk, I got to process and release emotions that I was feeling. In each walk, I learned that I can push my body through tough situations. In each walk, I learned that I am a good person, and I see the good in other people. In each walk, I learned that I was indeed a bad-ass training for a freaking half marathon at almost 300 pounds! In each walk, I learned that I am enough. Each step in each walk was in the direction of knowing that I am worthy. In each walk, I learned to love myself again.

And with that, I started hitting the pavement again. This time, instead of training for a half marathon (which technically I still was), I was loving myself. If Facebook was around, I would have changed my status to "In a Relationship with Walking" because that was my focus. I walked 4-8 miles every day throughout the week for the next month, and even a 10 mile walk the week before race day. I was on a high of *love*. I knew if I could walk 10 miles, I could walk 13.1 miles. I knew I would finish this race, and my heart was beaming!

Race Day was a very spiritual day for me. I was beyond anxious as I was in a space with thousands of other people I didn't know. Still, once I started breathing and looking around, I realized we were all there with a collective purpose to walk *our* race. What that is for each person is totally different, but it filled my heart with so much love for everyone around me because if they were feeling what I was feeling, there was nothing but love and excitement on that beach that day.

Showing up to a starting line is powerful in itself. You are challenging yourself to achieve a goal which means you are brave, you are strong, and you believe in your inner bad-assness! I felt that in my soul, and I felt that along the course. The race was tough mentally. I went through so many ups and downs, but I kept reminding myself that my training was enough, I am enough, and I deserve to see this race through.

It wasn't until I saw the 10-mile marker that I completely broke down crying like a baby. I knew if I could make it to 10 miles, I can make it to 13.1 miles. I cried for the entire 3.1 miles to the finish line, where my life was forever changed. Crossing that finish line taught me that if I can train for a half marathon, complete that half marathon, walk myself out of depression, and step into the ultimate form of self-love at the same time, I can do *anything*.

The best part of this story is that love is contagious, so I took this lesson taught to me and turned it into my own passion for helping women empower and love themselves at any size through fitness. I believe moving our bodies in joyful movements allows you to get to know yourself inside and out and realize the beautiful being that you are and how to love and care for the vessel that holds it. Walking is therapy and the gateway drug to stepping into self-love, and I am more than blessed to be the dealer.

Megan Sampson is a body positive personal trainer. She helps plus size women begin their fitness journeys in a safe and joyful manner. Her passion is self-love and empowerment. You can reach Megan at exermysize.com.

Here Comes The Judge
By Elaissia Sears

One could say that I am a reluctant politician. As a child, I remember looking out of the car window as I drove around with my parents during the election season and seeing campaign signs line the intersections. To me, the signs were meaningless. I thought to myself, "None of this matters. I will *never* run for office." It's striking that an elementary school student, raised in a safe neighborhood, would have such a jaded perspective. You see, I was a Black child born in the 90s, raised in the predominantly white suburb of Mesa, Arizona.

Mesa is where the first recorded retaliatory hate crime took place after 9/11. Not far from my house, a 52-year-old man, Balbir Singh Sodhi, a small-business owner and member of the Sikh community, was gunned down while planting flowers in honor of 9/11 victims. Mesa is also home to former legislator Russell Pearce, the politician behind Senate Bill SB1070, which gave law enforcement the authority to pull a person over based on the color of their skin. Notoriously racist Sheriff Joe Arpaio abused this law to terrorize communities of color across Arizona. Mesa has also made headlines for several incidents of police brutality. Seeing these injustices go unaddressed by our elected leaders repeatedly has an impact on Arizonans.

In 2017, I was a college-aged adult working full-time in the Arizona House of Representatives as a legislative assistant. I begrudgingly took the position as a favor, as I wanted nothing to do with our corrupt local government. I immediately began looking for an exit. I leveraged my network of legislators and changemakers. I set up informational interviews to explore where I could make a meaningful impact in a leadership role. Many suggested I run for a seat in the House, which I had no interest in.

One day, I went down to the Capitol lawn to observe the festivities for African American Legislative Day. Buses of Black children unloaded at the Capitol to take tours, perform dances, and listen to keynote speakers. One bus stood out, as it wasn't yellow but gray. Kids of all shades, no older than 14, were dressed neatly in beige uniforms and setting up chairs for the event. My eyes locked on a boy with a tattoo above his eyebrow. In my spirit, I sensed that something was wrong. A nearby legislator was watching as well. I asked her, "Where are all these kids from? Why are they setting up chairs?"

"They're from the kid prison." My heart dropped. The kid prison? My mother, the first person of color to serve on the Mesa Public Schools Governing Board, happened to be at the Capitol that day. With tears in my eyes, I ran over to her and told her what I had witnessed. "How can we stop this?" I passionately asked her. She looked at me lovingly, in a way only a mother can and said, "You can run for Justice of the Peace."

"What?!" I exclaimed. "That's for old white men."

"No, it's not. You can do it too."

I thought she was completely out of her mind. Then again, people told her the same thing when she ran for office. Yet, she did—and won by a landslide. I immediately began researching to learn more. Simultaneously, Mesa became the first city in Arizona with a private prison contract. Knowing that the path to mass incarceration starts in preschool, I knew I had to take a stand. When sharing my aspirations with other legislators, I was often met with ignorance and doubt. Still, I didn't let that hold me back.

One afternoon as I was canvassing for Justice of the Peace, I was near the end of my list of houses to visit. I knocked, and to my surprise, a Black woman opened the door.

"Hi! My name is Elaissia Sears, and I'm running for West Mesa Justice of the Peace."

"Oh! That's amazing! I didn't expect to see somebody like you at my door. Let me get my kids."

Three young Black children came to the door. She looked at them and said, "This woman is running for office, and she lives down the street from us!" The older boy looked surprised, the little girl excited, and the younger boy seemed disturbed. He looked at his mother and asked, "Her?! How can she be running for office? She looks like a kid!" I laughed. Although I'd been met with this comment hundreds of times, I continued giving my spiel. The children all listened intently, but he still wasn't convinced. "There's no way." He shook his head. "You can't do it." I thought there must be a reason why he thought this and asked him to explain why he felt this way. His brow furrowed, and he looked down. "I see that bad man on TV. Donald Trump. People voted for him, and he is horrible. I'm never going to vote."

I was saddened, but I understood. He reminded me of my younger self. "They don't care about us anyway." His mother turned to him and said, "This is why we have to vote. Look at her. She looks just like us. If we don't vote, she can't win." He peered into my eyes. "Well, I hope you can do it."

"We will. I promise."

A couple months later, I was elected at 24 years old as the youngest Justice of the Peace in Arizona. Despite the racist, ageist, sexist attacks from those who opposed my candidacy—including a white, middle-aged man who had held the position for 16 years. I won in a landslide, picking up 7,465 votes. Now, Mesa has a total of two Black elected officials—my mom and me! Also, thanks to our passion, instead of setting up chairs, those children are now participants in the African American Legislative Day.

I want children to look up to me and see that being a leader in the community is an attainable goal, no matter their appearance. Leadership doesn't have to be in the political arena. However, we are desperate for equal representation when only 5% of the Arizona population is Black. Children should know they can be whoever they want, and they don't need permission to share their greatness with the world. I want them to know I believe in them, and they are loved. I'm glad I was able to keep my promise. Our brilliance will not be dimmed by a country that only wanted to see us in chains.

Judge Elaissia Sears took office in January 2019 as Justice of the Peace for the West Mesa Justice Court. A graduate of Arizona State University, Judge Sears holds a B.A. in

Global Studies, a minor in German, and certificates in Political Entrepreneurship, Women and Gender Studies, and International Relations. She believes in creating equitable solutions within our court systems and fostering a positive relationship with the community. In her spare time, you can find her traveling the world with her husband, Sowan, and their two dogs Lil Boi and Yvonne. You may contact her at searsforjustice@gmail.com.

Now Let's Compare Our Magic Wands
By Lisa Sterne

It's 2020. I am 42 years old. My nine-year-old daughter, Lily, interrupts my writing with a request to join her in "HQ."

HQ is the fort we've developed in the living room. It's got pillows and blankets, an iPad for note-keeping and rules, and plenty of colorful strings hung from all sides, to attract one of the cats.

It wasn't like this a few months ago. The quarantine hit us fast and hard. Schools were shuttered, and a way of life changed in an instant. Sometimes, in the quiet moments, Lily cries. She misses her teachers, her friends, and her routine. "It happened fast," she tells me. I hug her, "Life does that sometimes," I say, "but you're making it through."

She has made it through a lot. Epilepsy will do that to you. It forces you to accept that you don't have full control and mastery of your body and life, and a joyful lesson it's not. But it's a good lesson. It's a sound one. It teaches faith, hope, and resilience.

I didn't want this diagnosis for her. When she was born, in all her sweet perfection, I envisioned a life of lightness and bliss.

Why do we do this?

I've yet to meet someone who tells me their life has been nothing but "lightness and bliss." It's the silliest and most reckless type of thinking there is.

Life brings hardships. It just does.

No matter how much we clench our fists and our teeth and hope for it not to, inevitably, hardships find us.

We can lean in. We can roll with them. We can face our fears by dancing along with the music of pain. And sadness. Despair. And grief.

Sometimes those emotions roll over me in such rapid succession that I become the most unevolved version of myself. Sometimes I watch those emotions bring Lily from 9 to 78.

"Sometimes life sucks," I whispered in her ear at the children's hospital. "Heard ya, Mommy!" she shouted back. We laughed. I'm not allowed to curse. That is why in those precious moments, I do.

"Sometimes life is such a jerk, and it makes us feel all buzzy and tense and angry," I tell her, "but then? You get through it. Tired and drained, for sure, but you get through it. Every. Single. Time. This is your superpower."

When they're little, we focus so much on reading and writing, social skills, and manners. But what about wisdom? Wisdom is how souls speak to one another. Wisdom teaches survival, humor, levity, and strength. I teach her wisdom.

She teaches me, childhood. She reminds me to build forts and make art and scream at the top of my lungs in the pool.

She laughs at mom jokes. She forces me to be present. She accepts nothing less than my best mom days and my worst ones.

One night, I had a weird feeling in the deepest part of my soul. "We were sisters before," I said aloud. I stood in stunned silence, and let the words fall out of my mouth, "We were sisters, in some other life. I don't know how I know this, but I do. When we play and scream and laugh like crazy in the pool, I suddenly remember."

I keep going, "I waited 33 years, in this life, to have her back. And when she got here, and I saw epilepsy and the gifted mind and disenchanted academic performance, I cried. Not just in the way that parents grieve a special needs diagnosis. I cried because I was sad that she had more challenges than she had 'last' time."

I let the wailing sobs wash over me. I trusted that my intuition was guiding me and that this was real.

"Mom, look. Look how I just decorated my craft box. Remember when I first got this craft kit, and I didn't know what to do with it? And then one day, suddenly, an idea just bites you in the butt!

Now, let's compare our magic wands."

Lisa Sterne obtained a BA in Psychology and Cognitive Science from Rutgers University, an MA in Professional Counseling from Monmouth University, and an MA in Organizational Psychology from Argosy University. She has worked as a therapist with children and families, in administration in nonprofit fundraising, and as boots on the ground in social justice activism. She is married, has a nine-year-old daughter, and three cats.

Instagram @healingspacesphx
lisakath@gmail.com

I Was Born In A Small Town
Katie Tryba

I hope many of you are like me and cannot get through reading this title without singing it. Thank you, John Mellencamp!

I think growing up in a small town can be a unique experience, because everybody knows everybody (another good song). I just cannot stop singing! Plus, it takes some imagination to entertain yourself. I am from Merrill, Wisconsin, the "City of Parks." Growing up, things that were consistent in my small-town life were attending church, showing up to local events, playing sports, going to school, enjoying nature, and spending time with family and friends.

For entertainment, we were lucky to have a bowling alley, movie theater, and the annual fair. One of our town's most quirky attractions was a team of female pig wrestlers, wearing wedding dresses, getting down and dirty in the mud. We would go to Chip's fast food restaurant, which has been there since the 60s, for delicious charbroiled burgers, curly fries with nacho cheese, and shakes. As teenagers, since this was right before GPS in the early 2000s, we would meet in Chip's parking lot with friends and follow each other to the parties. Partaking in this might earn you the nickname, "Chipper."

I know every small town probably says this, but we played hard in all of our sports. I like to believe we gave a little competition even to the bigger cities. High school football games were an important town event, they were always packed! I learned so much about myself from growing up playing basketball and softball. I was very fond of my traveling basketball coach, Marty. I had him as a coach from sixth grade through summers in high school. He taught us the basketball foundations and how important it was to play as a team, which made every player valuable. Sometimes he yelled, as do all coaches, but he mostly taught us with respect and kindness, which made us want to play hard for him. Traveling with my teammates for those weekend tournaments was always an adventure that brought us closer together. Sometimes we got into mischief. I remember once we were exploring between games, running through the woods next to the school, we ran across a log to cross a creek, and I fell in with my basketball shoes on. To say the least, they were not thrilled about me playing the rest of the day in soggy, wet, squeaky shoes.

All through high school, I had pretty good coaches for all of my sports. One year a good chunk of my basketball team was going away to an out-of-town basketball camp for the week. My mom, being a single parent, said we couldn't afford it, and the high school basketball coaches decided to pitch in to send me with the team. They'll never know how grateful I was for that, and I remember crying tears of joy for their generosity.

There was a strong sense of community at the church in our town. When bumming around town with friends, there were extra eyes everywhere, making sure I was safe, which I appreciate now. I learned how important it is to volunteer and to give back to others. It didn't matter that I came home stinking of fish fries after volunteer waitressing for Lent.

This might seem strange in lots of other states, but in Wisconsin, there are lots of bars and churches in each town. In fact, we have so many bars that we rank as one of the highest states with the most bars per capita! When you say "Old Fashioned," it's not a style, every Wisconite knows to ask for brandy or whiskey and sweet or sour. As a teenager, I always thought it was gross when my parents drank Old Fashioneds, but here I love them, and they always make me nostalgic for home.

As a student, it felt good to feel cared for by your teachers, counselors, coaches, and the rest of the school staff. To this day, I can recall the sweetness and joy of my third-grade teacher. It was neat to see your teachers outside of school. I had a math teacher and high school counselor that would referee our basketball games. It gave us something in common we could joke or talk trash about. Once, I broke a finger playing basketball, and a student in my math class slammed my hand with a book to get my attention. Normally it wouldn't have hurt, but considering my finger was broken, I screamed out loud in pain, and it brought tears to my eyes. My math teacher hollered at the student and sent them out. The student apologized. I didn't have a bandage on, so they didn't know and were just trying to tease me. It wasn't a big deal, but I remember feeling safe and appreciated that the teacher had my back.

I'll never forget how I got my first job at 15 as a grocery store cashier. On a very hot summer day, my basketball coach and I painted the entrance of the store. I remember between the heat and paint fumes, I got sick in the bathroom (my coach didn't realize). I was grateful and needed the job, so I kept painting until it was done.

As I mentioned, Merrill is the City of Parks, so we have beautiful spots all over to be outside and bodies of water for fun. We loved boating on the Wisconsin river and always visited this tiny island to jump off the old rope swing. I hear my nieces in high school today talking about the rope swing, and it feels like a rite of passage.

All these little moments really do add up in one child's life and make a lasting impression. Be good to your schools, community, and just one another, as it really does take a village's love to raise someone. They will be all the better to pay forward your love to someone else.

Katie Tryba is from central Wisconsin. She is a graduate student finishing her masters to be a clinical mental health counselor. Her background includes teaching special education, facilitating at a day treatment for children and adolescents, volunteer sexual assault advocate, and short stories author. She is passionate about helping others heal. You can reach Katie at tryba.katie+book@gmail.com.

Love Now More Than Ever
By Amanda Uzzardo

When I signed up for this project, it was going to be an inspiring story of true, unconditional love and how it can contribute to personal healing and growth. I wanted to express how much my wife means to me and how much she inspires me. I wanted to highlight how she's taught me to love unconditionally and how that love has given me the power to face the world. Even though loving unconditionally makes us vulnerable, the benefits outweigh the potential negatives of vulnerability.

However, the weight on my heart compels me to use this important opportunity to highlight how love is needed now more than ever. There is so much hate and oppression that needs to be overcome, but love will help power the necessary changes. My goal is to inspire unbiased, whole-hearted, and unrestricted love in our communities.

Throughout my adolescence, I was taught this "PG" version of historical events. I was also taught racism is not a real problem, but more of an exaggeration in our minds to have someone to blame other than ourselves for our problems. Imagine my surprise going out into the real world and realizing that racism and oppression are realities. For years, I would tune out the ugly and focus on the rainbows in the world. Rainbows are easier to face and make me happy. I had somehow convinced myself if I don't see a problem, then it doesn't exist.

A class on multiculturalism opened my eyes to the world's historical injustices. Things have changed over time, but can we honestly say they've improved? So many people see change and think it means things are getting better. What they don't realize is that change does not equal better. Not to discredit the progress that has been made, but if circumstances are not improved for those who need it most, then is it really progress or just diverting attention from injustices that still exist? I was ashamed to realize just how blind I had been. Spending a semester learning about racism and oppression tore my rainbow glasses from my face. It forced me to recognize the injustice existing in the world around me. That class made me realize not recognizing and acknowledging racism and oppression is actually contributing to the problem.

Seeing the world without my rainbow glasses terrified me. I am raising two strong-minded and even stronger-willed young Black Mexican American men and the world is an incredibly dangerous place for people of color. Every time I read a story about someone pleading for their life or being murdered because of the color of their skin, I wonder how their loved ones must feel. I think about the pain and anger they must feel. Something inside of you, as a human being, should be aching from the sadness and injustice of it all. How could you not recognize the need for change?

We are raising two amazing sons who believe in magic, miracles, and the power of laughter and love. Our sons recognize the importance of living by the golden rule and the power of kindness. They also see the world through rainbow glasses. They aspire to be doctors, restaurant owners, engineers, or designers depending on the day. Still, you will never know this if you can't see past the color of their skin. As they grow older, how do I replace their fairytales with the truth about racism and oppression? At what age do we have to switch from sheltering our children from the hate in the world to protecting them by preparing them to face it? How do I take away their bright-eyed childhood innocence when I have to explain to them that even though they love and respect everyone, one day, they may encounter someone who will judge them and hate them based solely on the color of their skin? I hope when they do encounter that hateful person, that it is not a person of authority.

We shouldn't have to prepare our children to always show their hands and reassure others that they do not pose a threat. The sad truth is that we must because our sweet innocent boys will one day grow up to be strong Black Mexican American men. Not everyone will get to know them before hating them or perceiving them as a threat. *It is not right!* It should not be my children's responsibility to help you see your insecurities are inaccurate. It should not be their responsibility to defend the color of their skin. It is your responsibility to educate yourself and recognize that someone's color is not a reason to judge or hate them.

We have to be able to love and respect one another. We have to be seen for who we are rather than the color of our skin. We have to acknowledge and honor our differences rather than let them divide us. We need to stand up and fight for the rights of our fellow human beings. Racism, inequality, and human rights are everyone's battle to fight, even if you are not impacted by them directly.

I may not have all of the answers, and I may not even recognize the true size of this fight, but I recognize the need for change. We can start with wholehearted love and support for one another. I may not be black, but I recognize that Black Lives Matter and my heart is broken. How do you ignore the pain, tears, and blood of our black community? To help our hearts heal, we have to be able to believe; believe in the power of being part of the change that is so necessary, believe in the power of equality, and believe in the power of love.

Amanda Uzzardo is a proud love rebel. She believes in fighting for equality with the power of love.

A Reflection In Self Love
By Cherrie Vierra-Lonkar

Mine is a story of reflection. Cancer and motherhood, and everything I wish I'd known. It's interesting how your approach can change based on necessity and preservation of sanity. When I was a new mother, I had four babies all at once, thanks to becoming a foster/adoptive parent and a surprise pregnancy. They were our multi-hued "quads," our fab four. When they were babies, my life was a well-oiled machine. They often wore coordinating outfits, complete with handmade bows for my daughter's piggy tails. I always knew where their bottles/sippy cups were. They were also color-coded to ensure that someone didn't get the wrong kind of formula. They always ate a hot breakfast as they sat in their row of highchairs. My house was always tidy and company ready, largely due to the strategic configuration of gates that kept the babies and their vast array of toys corralled in one area of the house. I got dressed and did my makeup nearly every day. I always had a diaper bag fully stocked and ready to go. I, like most moms of high order multiples, rarely took them out on weekdays unless it was for a doctor's appointment. Outings were always done on weekends when I had Daddy to help. There was the rare emergency when I'd have to line their baby car seats on a flatbed at Costco and drag them through the store as people stared. The thought of meeting girlfriends at Chick-fil-A for the kids to play was met with a, "Thanks for the invite. Maybe next time." The thought of them picking up germs at the play center and getting each other sick was overwhelming. Not because I was a germaphobe, but because of how my world was rocked when caring for four babies that were sick at the same time. My system worked. It allowed me to live in the ideal that I had created for myself while maintaining sanity and keeping anxiety at bay. I would often worry that I was too rigid or not social enough. I often doubted myself.

Fast forward to today. My face easily goes three weeks without makeup. Jude, our youngest, is a free-range toddler in a house nearly twice the size. This means that my house typically looks like it sneezed the makings of epic toddler exploration. Not to mention that I can rarely find the sippy cup that he started the day with. What's Jude's color? Yellow. However, most of his cups have pink lids because they are his sisters' handed down princess cups because his countless Thomas the Train cups have fallen victim to the toddler abyss. Jude often wears his pajamas for the day because we are just hanging out at home between toting the big kids to and from. It's not uncommon for Jude to eat a fruit/veggie pouch for breakfast while he cranes his neck in his rear-facing car seat in an attempt to see the Disney movie that is playing while we shuttle his big kids to school. I almost never have a diaper bag packed. Rather, I choose to play a game of backseat roulette. That's where I gamble on the assumption that there *has* to be a pack of diapers, wipes, and a pair of shoes that have been tossed somewhere in the back of the car. We have very few toys by comparison.

My world has broadened since those early years of motherhood. My confidence has grown, and I've learned lessons every single day. My life and relationships are vastly different. Now, we have space for spontaneous playdates and coffee shop meetups. We play harder. We invest more of ourselves in the people that we love who reside outside of our walls. I have room to pick up a girlfriend's slack and the confidence to let them pick up mine. I no longer have room for perfection. Life hasn't allowed it. At some point, all of us moms will have to face a day when our lives no longer accommodate our need for perfection, control, or overachievement. For some of you, it won't be until your only child is in college. For others, it may be when life throws you a curveball in the form of a surprise baby, a divorce, or an illness. In the thick of it, I know it feels heavy, fraught, and an inch away from ruining your kids. But, hang on because you will settle in, and so will your kids. The shift in values will happen slowly, and at times it will feel like emotional arthritis in its ache. But, once you turn the corner, you exhale and realize your kids are happy, joyful souls who are still shining. I'm certain there will be more corners to turn and an infinite number of lessons that motherhood has in store for me. But today, I sit in a moment that tells me it's all going to be okay. I hope your heart can read this and allow you to cut yourself some slack. Love yourself and where you are at. You are doing just fine.

My hope is that you embrace the message that loving yourself and honoring where you are is critical to your happiness and well-being. Love yourself and hold space for not only the person who you are today but the person you will become. You are enough.

Cherrie Vierra-Lonkar is a counselor, educator, and the Executive Director at Branching Out Family Services. She supports families within the special needs and foster-adoptive communities grow, connect, and thrive. She is passionate about empowering those who are often overlooked.

Cherrie can be reached at:
www.BranchingOutFamilyServices.com
480-757-1002
Cherrie@BranchingOutFamilyServices.com

Love Is A Cliché
By Cam Vuksinich

Let us begin with an uncomfortable truth: we are hostages, and love has been hijacked. It needs to be said, and I was afraid to say it until now. I will no longer let fear coerce my silence. It is time for an uprising, a time to elevate the standing of love in our hearts and in the world.

Cliché: a saying or an idea which has been so overused it has lost its power. Love is a word shared by priests, poets, artists, and playwrights for millennia to influence and inspire the masses. Still, it has never been as exploited as it is now for commercial purposes. Did you know that love is one of the most common words found in advertising? When I googled the phrase "love used for advertising," the search revealed over 2,000,000,000 results—that is trillion with a T. Love, one of life's most precious experiences, is wielded daily by marketers to sell us cars, vacations, hamburgers, and dog food. It is no wonder when asked, "What is love?" our answers are vague, unclear, fuzzy, and confusing. Yet, we know in the depth of our souls, without love, life is meaningless. The challenge of reclaiming love may feel like a herculean task. Yet, this rite of passage may be exactly what the world needs, a timely revelation of our destiny.

Why did I choose the topic? One word, rebel: a term that was used to describe me by those who value conformity. The memory of catholic school and the "daily kneel," not an act of reverence in a church but a requirement in school to make sure the girls' skirts touched the floor. Instead of allowing it to curb my rebellious impulse, I seized the opportunity to live an exciting life with the intent to leave a memorable legacy. Which leads me to my next thought, stirring the pot.

Picture a pot of soup. A lot of ingredients have settled to the bottom, out of sight, until stirred. A lot of issues can remain hidden from view yet will exert an unseen influence. One can "stir the pot" to bring issues to the surface to raise awareness and affect change. Time for all of us to grab a big spoon!

In stirring the pot, I hope to start a conversation. I have been fascinated by the idea of love for as long as I can remember and often struggled to define, describe, or even say the word. Love evokes emotions, memories, and is easily misunderstood. Face it. Love is scary. I have met countless people who feel the same discomfort, confusion, and fear when love is expressed. I wondered how this simple four-letter word could elicit such a powerful reaction. I stirred and stirred, and finally, an answer appeared; love is missing a vital ingredient, power. I felt the underlying truth of this goosebump moment but did not quite understand the depth of the revelation. I became fixated on the idea of power.

Power. A five-letter word that exerts itself into the conversation. Historically, power has been bestowed, stolen, or commanded. Its nature wields influence, impact, and control. It catalyzes action. (Grab a spoon, we're getting ready to stir the pot again.) In researching the most powerful leaders of all time, except for a few notable women, the vast majority are men. This introduces another uncomfortable truth: men claimed power, not necessarily by intention, but through cultural norms. Since power was not available for women, what was their domain? Why love, of course! To continue to preserve the transfer of power to males, the justification is that women became known as the weaker sex, which in turn perpetuated the impotency of love. This exposes the nature of another uncomfortable truth: love has been unnaturally separated from power, and power has been unnaturally separated from love. The duality of this misfortune is clear. Power without love is force. Love without power is weakness. How do we heal this ill-fated misunderstanding? The solution is chemistry.

Let us return to Chemistry 101. A scientific definition of "solution" is a homogeneous mixture of two or more substances that has the same proportions of its components throughout. In other words, mix equal parts power with love. Love was never meant to be excluded from power, and power was never meant to be separated from love. We could imagine it as empowered love. This next step will require a change of heart, not an organ transplant, but a shift in perception.

We do not need to understand something to experience its impact, for example, gravity. The most brilliant minds have no idea what it is or how it works, but not one of us can deny its power. The gravitational power of love may keep us firmly grounded as we face the daily challenges of preserving the best of human nature: the undeniable urge for the communion of belonging. It's time to correct the misperception that love can be removed from power. It is like trying to separate the air you breathe from the life you live.

Are you willing to challenge beliefs that render love weak and power cruel? Are you willing to speak up when you notice how the culture of politics, religion, consumerism, or personal relationships negatively impact the nature of love? Are you willing to rebel against a status quo that suggests love is buying the next car, taking a trip, or eating a hamburger? Are you willing to consider that you may already be equal parts love and power?

One final thought, words matter. For instance, names that work at a company's launch do not always work as the company evolves. In fact, the original name might be an obstacle to growth. Here is a bit of trivia: Google was once named BackRub. Need I say more? It is time to distinguish empowered love from its commercialized cousin by adopting all upper-case letters to emphasize its true nature: LOVE. It's time.

My name is Cam Vuksinich. Every day for the last 30 years, I wake up filled with gratitude. I love what I do for a living. As a Holistic Life Coach, I support clients as they navigate the uncertain moments of their life. I am guided by the belief that everyone has inner wisdom, and it is my job to listen and ask the right questions. They are the experts. I am a passionate ally. I also founded a non-profit, One World Heart Project, which is dedicated to recognizing the power of the smallest acts of love.

www.creativeinsightscoaching.com
www.oneworldheartproject.org.

Where's My Milkshake?
By Randy Walters

Shortly after I opened my first restaurant in 2008, I learned that not every customer who walked through the door was there for our home-cooked food. Many came seeking comfort. The comfort that comes when you sit among others, enjoying good food, laughter, and those typical diner sounds. Just people sharing a fun experience, knowing that if you are sitting alone at your table, you're still part of the collective group, dining at that moment.

That people came to restaurants for reasons other than filling their bellies was what I shared with every employee. And that every customer has a story, and whatever life handed them on any given day can affect their behavior. So, when you get that customer who is surly, angry, distant, or flat-out rude, always remember that they have a story. We are given the opportunity to show that customer kindness, love, and compassion, along with serving them amazing comfort food.

One late Friday afternoon, during our normal slow time between the lunch rush and dinner service, I got my most amazing opportunity yet to practice what I preached to my employees. I was sitting at our cashier's counter doing some doodling when the front door opened and in stepped an older gentleman, thin and slightly hunched over. He had a full head of wavy gray hair, a white dress shirt with the collar opened and a thin black tie, swinging loosely as he slowly lumbered toward me. Black pants and a black fedora held in front of him completed the look. I reached for a menu and greeted him with a friendly, "Welcome to Wimpy's Paradise, sir," to which he gave no reply. He sat with his back to me, placed his fedora on the seat next to him, and put both hands, open-palmed, over his eyes, and let out a very pronounced sigh. As I made my way to his table, I set the menu in front of him and asked if he'd eaten here before. His reply was, "Give me a hamburger, no cheese." His face was still covered by his hands. "Anything to drink, sir?" I asked, and again in a short, gruff answer, he said, "No!" Of all the customers who I had experienced, I sensed the gentleman was making it quite clear that he wanted no small talk, just a burger with no cheese.

I took his ticket back to the kitchen, repeated to the cook, "Burger, no cheese," and returned to sit at the cashier's counter. The gentleman's back was to me, and I studied his behavior. He was softly strumming his fingers on the tabletop and quietly mumbling to himself. At times, he would look across the table, then give a heavy sigh and lower his eyes to his busy fingers. I felt so helpless, and I wanted to speak with him, to see if I could, in some small way, cheer him up. However, he made it abundantly clear that he didn't want to be bothered.

Then, the order-up bell rang from the kitchen, and I picked up the burger, utensils, and napkin and started towards my only customer. He leaned back as I set his burger, silverware, and napkin down, and I asked him if there was anything else that I could get him. Without looking up at me, he said angrily, "Where's my milkshake?" He had never ordered a milkshake, but I said to him, "Sir, I forgot what flavor shake you ordered." "Chocolate!" he yelled back. So, I walked away to make him a chocolate shake. I brought him his shake in our traditional milkshake glass, which was a tall, old fashioned soda fountain glass. I was soon going to find out just how important that presentation was to him. "Here's your shake, sir," I said as I set it on his table. He reached for it and said nothing. I stepped away, uncertain if I would ever be able to show this gentleman any light or hope in what seemed to be a dark day for him. I watched as he slowly finished his burger and ever so slowly got to the bottom of the shake. Then, I heard the sound that we all love to hear. The straw sucking the last of that delicious chocolate shake. That was my signal. Time to accept the fact that sometimes, people may not be ready to see the light at that moment. Sometimes, they just want to be left to process and deal with whatever is hurting them, or maybe, just maybe, he was comfortable in being a private, surly, angry old man.

As I brought the man his check, I told him that I didn't charge him for the milkshake since it was my fault that I "forgot" which flavor he had ordered. I asked him how his burger was, and for the first time, he looked up at me. His eyes were bloodshot and watery. He gave me a little smile and said, "My wife would have loved this place." It was then that I had a glimpse into this man's story. I asked if I could sit down at the table. "Please do," he responded. I asked him, already knowing the answer, "Where's your wife?" Our eyes met, and he said, "I just buried her, and it was just our pastor and me. In fact, this is my first meal without her in 55 years." I was now feeling a hint of his pain. "Please tell me about your wife," and for the next thirty minutes, he shared their love story, which included their first date, where they shared a chocolate shake.

As he stood to leave, we hugged, and he thanked me for the meal. As he turned to walk away, he said, "I love your place, but you do understand that I can never come back here." I replied, "I understand." His parting words were, "I will never forget your kindness or our chocolate shake."

Randy Walters, Chandler, AZ. please contact me with questions or comments at Damillhunk22@yahoo.com.

Being The Change
By Caroline Wright

As I finally sit down to write my excerpt for this book that ought to be based on love, I am met with an overwhelming feeling of sadness. While I will try to make this brief, as I only have a couple of pages, I do want to set the stage a bit.

My God, I feel as if I'm writing some fiction novel about a time in the distant past or far into the future.

But I'm not. This is somehow real life.

We are currently at a crossroads. A major pandemic has swept the globe, and no, we're not in the clear. A massive outcry for social justice and equal rights has created a way for government-ordered curfews. A month ago, I had to explain what a "ration" was to my sweet little blonde-haired, blue-eyed five-year-old son. A few days ago, I had to justify why I was a "social media activist" rather than being at the peaceful protests myself.

The reason, you ask? The reason I "hide" behind a computer or phone to convey my message?

The reason is this:

> I am a mother of two strong little boys. They are two and five years old. Both of their fathers have dealt with addiction in the past. And, on the off chance that something was to happen to me? Their fathers would be deemed their providers. Now, while they are currently succeeding in their roads to recovery and have been sober for some time now,

my maternal instinct jumps to the times ingrained in my memory in which their addiction changed them beyond recognition. Though I wholeheartedly believe in their success, I fear that my death would trigger something within them that would dominate their logic and send them spiraling, leaving my sweet, impressionable little men to live a life that would not be best for them.

I don't want this life. I want so much more for them—and myself—and every living being around me.

However, wanting change through methods of activism is so often frowned upon.

"It's all for nothing," they say.

"What will it change?" they implore.

"Why do you care so much? You aren't black."

You're right. I am not black.

I am not anything but some random European-descended mutt whose skin turns a lovely shade of cherry red in the summer sun.

There was a time in my life that I wore a hijab, the Muslim headscarf. It was during this time that I was harassed with statements like, "You're a fucking terrorist piece of shit" (I'm not), "*You're* not that white boy's mother" (I am), and "Go back to where you came from."

Sure, I'll go back to Orange County, California. Are you paying for my rent, or...?

Fast-forward to now, I am loaded up with tattoos, love to express myself through my clothing, and have short hair.

And now? I'm deemed "too punk" (I'm not), "too controversial" (okay, maybe I'll give you that one), "too gay-looking" (yes, this has been said to me).

And so, I've come to realize this. There is prejudice everywhere. If you don't fit the status quo, you're bound to have someone trying to vote you off the island.

But I'm learning something else. I'm becoming increase-ingly aware that I do have a slight advantage, even with my tattoos and short hair and the fact that I sometimes sport a button-up shirt.

With that pale, easily-burnt skin, comes a voice. And though women "should be" prim and proper, gentle, calm, and a plethora of other demoting adjectives, we as humans overall are so much louder when we step out of the box that society has man-handled us into.

We are one. We bleed the same blood. We have no future without love.

And mind you, what I've written thus far is not necessarily meant to be a call to action. However, if you feel that it is, may I suggest that you take a moment to reflect on your inner workings and the mentality that you have been taught over the years?

No, this is just me. Venting. Processing. Coming to terms with the fact that life is far more unpredictable and more uncanny than anyone could ever have prepared me for.

But one thing is for sure—through all of it, I will choose to love myself, and those around me to whatever capacity I can and teach my children and any future generations that love will somehow overcome.

Maybe these words will be met by someone exploring what love means to them. Maybe it will be met by someone open to change or acceptance that they never previously imagined they would have.

Here's where I insert my suggested call-to-action:

Go be the change. Go be the love in this often-cruel world. Stand up for those without a voice. Learn to love who you are, right now. Flaws and all, for not a single one of us is perfect. Love in all facets of the word. Eradicate prejudice and revolt against oppression. Choose love every single day, in every single interaction.

Please.

Just love.

Caroline Wright is a mother, musician, and artist living near Phoenix, Arizona. To view her art and learn about her, visit www.instagram.com/carolinewrightart. There you will find links to several different ventures she has begun.

Final Thoughts

I am grateful for each and every one of you, fifty-three authors who were brave enough, courageous enough to share love in the world. When the world can seem dark, it is all of you who inspire me to continue to keep loving myself and others. Thank you for being brave enough to express who you are and share the essence of who we are in this transformative book. Thank you for choosing love.

Tara Ijai
Love Glasses Revolution
Myloveglasses.com

Made in the USA
Monee, IL
03 November 2020